Columbia University

Contributions to Education

Teachers College Series

No. 44

AMS PRESS
NEW YORK

THE EDUCATIONAL VIEWS AND INFLUENCE OF DEWITT CLINTON

BY

EDWARD A. FITZPATRICK, M.A., Ph.D.

TEACHERS COLLEGE, COLUMBIA UNIVERSITY
CONTRIBUTIONS TO EDUCATION, NO. 44

PUBLISHED BY
Teachers College, Columbia University
NEW YORK CITY
1911

Library of Congress Cataloging in Publication Data

Fitzpatrick, Edward Augustus, 1884-1960.
  The educational views and influence of DeWitt Clinton.

  Reprint of the 1911 ed., issued in series: Teachers
College, Columbia University. Contributions to edu-
cation, no. 44.
  Originally presented as the author's thesis, Columbia.

  Bibliography: p.
  1. Clinton, De Witt, 1769-1828. 2. Education--New
York (State)--History. I. Title. II. Series:
Columbia University. Teachers College. Contributions
to education, no. 44.
LB695.C6F5 1972   370'.92'4   78-176775
  ISBN 0-404-55044-4

Reprinted by Special Arrangement with Teachers
College Press, New York, New York

From the edition of 1911, New York
First AMS edition published in 1972
Manufactured in the United States

AMS PRESS, INC.
NEW YORK, N.Y. 10003

PREFACE

The history of education in the United States has yet to be written—and the first big step in the process is the completion of a series of the educational history of the individual states. The present study is a contribution to the history of education in the State of New York, during the period of foundations, or rather, during the period of the transformation of the English colonial character—and consequently education—to a distinctly American one. This study centers about the rich personality of one of New York's greatest sons—De Witt Clinton. His educational significance has received very slight recognition from his biographers. Though he is not mentioned in either of the histories of education in the United States, and though mentioned, is not adequately treated, in any of the histories of education in New York State this study establishes, we believe, the claim that Clinton should be ranked with Mann and Barnard in a trinity of educational leadership in the United States. Preceding the study of De Witt Clinton, there is, by way of introduction, a statement of the physical, social and educational conditions in the State of New York from 1783 to 1805.

The student of the educational history of Massachusetts is, in general, oppressed by the wealth of material. It would seem that whenever any one did anything educationally, there was a fellow-townsman nearby to record his work, or else he himself took the time later to record it. Consequently, the educational history of Massachusetts is, at present, the most complete. The student of the educational history of New York has just the opposite

iii

experience. He is oppressed by the scantiness of material. Governor Fenner, when he invited Henry Barnard to become State Superintendent of Education in Rhode Island, gave expression to what, unfortunately, may be called the New York view: that it was better to make history than write it.

The writer has quoted freely from the sources, especially in Chapter III. The reasons for this are: (1) the conclusions are so novel to the general reader or teacher that they would probably be dismissed merely as other illustrations of reading into things conclusions, which the things themselves would not warrant being read out of them; (2) the reader has the opportunity of forming his own conclusions; (3) the material quoted from is either bulky or generally inaccessible; and finally (4) there may be those like George Eliot, who prefer to "learn from the man himself what he thought, than hear from others what he ought to have thought."

The author wishes to acknowledge his obligations to the librarian of the Columbia University Library, the Bryson Library, Teachers College, the New York State Library, the New York City Library, the Library of the New York Historical Society, the Lenox and the Astor Foundations, and the branch libraries (especially the Hamilton Fish Branch) of the New York Public Library, and to the authorities of the New York State Education Department, for many kindnesses, courtesies, and privileges. He is under deep obligations to Dr. Paul Monroe, of Teachers College, Columbia University, for patient, kindly, and valuable criticism extending over several years' study. His greatest obligation is to his mother, who, through long years of sacrifice, made it possible for him to secure an education.

E. A. F.

CONTENTS

PART II

THE EDUCATIONAL VIEWS OF DE WITT CLINTON AND
THEIR SIGNIFICANCE

PART III

INFLUENCE OF DE WITT CLINTON AND ITS SIGNIFICANCE

INTRODUCTION

Mr. Edward A. Fitzpatrick, with whom I have no personal acquaintance, sent me the proof-sheets of his study of the relations of De Witt Clinton to American, and particularly to New York education, and asked me to comment upon his work. It is obviously impossible for one in my official position to assume such a task very often; indeed, I did not *assume* this one. But his subject is one of such peculiar interest to me that I could not refrain from reading enough to know whether he had written something worth reading, and thereupon found that what he had written was so well worth my reading that I read the whole of it.

Having done so, I can justly say no less than that the author has, in striving to do educational justice to the memory of De Witt Clinton, rendered a very substantial service to the history of education in the great state which Clinton served with so much distinction, and that of course means to the history of education in America. The work is not only marked by laborious research, but also by a confident grasp upon the general and widespread facts of educational history which is not often possessed by a young man in his college days.

He very appropriately portrays the New York educational situation as it existed in the last two decades of the eighteenth century and in the first decade of the nineteenth, in order to elucidate the educational activities which De Witt Clinton set in motion. This portrayal is doubtless more complete than the period has had at the hands of any previous writer. Educational facts have been gleaned not only from laws and official reports, but also from the newspapers and school announcements of the times and from other primary sources of information, until the work affords us a clearer view of the low state of education in New York a hundred years ago than any to which we have been accustomed.

This, however, is only the prelude to the real work of the author—that of showing Governor Clinton's strong grasp upon the sociological situation and his remarkable fertility of mind in seeing the remedies for it, as well as that of revealing his foresight, energy, and courage, and his commanding influence in compelling New York to take the steps which have given her educational eminence, thus entitling him to a yet higher place in our history because of what he did for learning than because of what he did in the building of the Erie Canal, with which his name has been most conspicuously identified.

I have, of course, read much in the history of New York education, and have not been wholly ignorant of the obligations under which it lies to De Witt Clinton, but it involves no humiliation to say that I have not heretofore appreciated the many-sidedness of his persistent activities for the intellectual progress of the state. I knew what he had said, many times and forcefully, in his state papers as Governor, but I had too much of the feeling that he had said it perfunctorily and because it was good political policy to say it. That was natural enough, as things ordinarily go, but Mr. Fitzpatrick's study shows that it was very unjust. The evidence here brought back to the light and assembled in a very systematic whole shows that at all times and places he worked sagaciously and incessantly to advance the moral and intellectual progress of his people, and, wholly apart from the other large things he did, is entitled to rank among the very first educational propagandists of America.

The young man who has made this apparent is entitled to and has the appreciative acknowledgments of the New York State Education Department.

A. S. DRAPER,
Commissioner of Education.

ALBANY, N. Y.,
July 17, 1911.

PART I

CONDITIONS IN NEW YORK STATE

1783-1805

CHAPTER I

PHYSICAL AND SOCIAL CONDITIONS

STATISTICS OF POPULATION

In 1800 New York was a sparsely settled frontier settlement—in no sense the empire state. The settlements already made were on two narrow oblongs extending north and east from New York City; the one north was forty miles in breadth and was divided by the Hudson; the one east was Long Island. On the 44,000 square miles there lived, according to the census of 1800, 586,050 people; of those 20,613 were slaves and 10,374 were included in the class of "all other persons except Indians not taxed."[1]

The population was almost entirely rural; there was an average of less than fourteen persons to the square mile.[2] There were but three incorporated cities: New York, Albany, and Hudson. New York City had a population of 32,328; Albany had but 3,498 and Hudson only 2,584. Western New York remained practically a wilderness—this fact is indicated on Morse's map of the State (1804) by the absence of any names of towns in that part of the State. A few settlers had gathered at Buffalo. Neither Rochester, Rome, nor Syracuse had any existence. Utica was insignificant. Schenectady had "decayed" since the Revolution and had not been rebuilt. Canandaigua, the chief town in Ontario County, contained seventy dwelling houses, and Geneva contained a like number. Bath, the chief town in Steuben County, contained but thirty houses,[3] and the enumeration of

---

[1] Pioneer Association of Genesee County. History of its organization, p. 20.

[2] For the relation between the growth of an urban population and the development of the graded school see Harris's monograph on Elementary Education *in* Butler's Education in the United States.

[3] P. 1183—"A description of the Genesee Country in the State of New York"; Document H, *in* O'Callaghan's Documentary History of New York.

the inhabitants in the town itself and the district eight miles around it, showed that there were "above eight hundred souls."[4] Steuben County had but 1,788 souls. There were seven other counties with less than ten thousand inhabitants. Richmond had 4,563; Kings, 5,740; Rockland, 6,353; Tioga, 6,889; Onandago, 7,406; Clinton and Essex Counties together, 8,514; and Schohary, 9,808. But very few counties had more than twenty-five thousand inhabitants. It is no wonder, then, that with such a scattered population, schools were not more adequately provided.

THE GROWTH OF POPULATION

But the growth of population is more significant than the fact of population. In 1790 the population of New York City was 33,131; in 1830 it was 197,112. In 1790 there was one city of over eight thousand inhabitants and the total urban population was 33,131; in 1830 there were seven cities of over eight thousand inhabitants with a total urban population of 271,481. The population of the state in 1790 was 340,120, and in 1830 it was 1,918,608. The increase of population in the State was considerably over fivefold (5.64); the increase of urban population was over eightfold (8.19).[5]

LACK OF READY AND COMFORTABLE MEANS OF COMMUNICATION AND TRANSPORTATION

Nor was this population welded closer together by easy and ready means of communication, or transportation. The stage coach was the usual means of land travel. A contemporary advertisement reads:

"Federal Line (of Stages) for Philadelphia will leave for New York every day at eight o'clock in the morning (Sundays excepted) and arrives at Philadelphia early next. Fare of each passenger, four dollars.

"Albany stages will leave New York every day at ten o'clock in the morning; arrives at Albany the fourth day at nine o'clock in the morning. Fare of each passenger, seven dollars."

---

[4] P. 1135—"Description of the Settlement of the Genesee Country in the State of New York in a series of letters from a gentleman to his friend" published *in* O'Callaghan's Documentary History of New York.

[5] Cf. Census Reports.

Roads were few and in exceedingly poor condition. Travel was expensive. The trip to Albany was less comfortable and less regular than the voyage to Europe. There was no Erie Canal. There were no steamboats and no railroads.[6]

CHARACTER OF NEWSPAPERS

Newspapers were not the significant social force that they are to-day. The newspapers at the end of the eighteenth century consisted almost entirely of advertisements and the "latest European intelligence." Advertisements occupied about half of the newspaper and, occasionally, two-thirds. The "latest European intelligence" was mostly political and was published at least two months after the facts occurred, occasionally taking the form of a detailed report of the debates in the British House of Commons. "The Spectator" published the debates in the United States Congress, giving over half of the paper to this department. Occasionally laws passed by Congress were published. Besides the foregoing, these eighteenth century newspapers contained long political discussions by "Scipio" and the like, quotations from a "late London paper," or other newspapers, or an extract from a letter from an American in Paris dated three months earlier. Surely there was little possibility in this material to arouse the people to an adequate conception of their social needs.[7]

THE SYSTEM OF POOR-RELIEF

One of the big problems connected with a rapid increase in population and especially of its concentration in rather small areas is poor-relief, with its usual development of beggars, criminals and the like. The system of administration of poor-relief was borrowed from England,[8] and it was accompanied here by the

---

[6]"The number of letters was almost one a year for every grown inhabitant in the United States." Adam's History of the United States, v. 1, p. 62.

[7]"Of American newspapers there was no end, but the education supposed to have been widely spread by eighteenth century newspapers was hardly to be distinguished from ignorance. The student of history might search forever these storehouses of political calumny for facts to instruct the public in any useful object." Adam's History of United States, v. 1, p. 120.

[8]"The principles of administration of poor relief laid down in the act of Elizabeth and modified by the Act of Charles II. remained practically un-

same evil results as there. The situation is clearly and sharply stated in the following rather long quotation from De Witt Clinton. It may be observed here in passing that his remedy, "intellectual, moral and religious cultivation," is not an English one.

"Our statutes relating to the poor are borrowed from the English system, and the experience of that country, as well as our own, shows that pauperism increases with the augmentation of the funds applied to its relief. This evil has proceeded to such an alarming extent in the City of New York, that the burden of heavy taxation which it has imposed, means a diminution of the population of that city, and a depreciation of its real property. The consequences will be very injurious to the whole State; for the delay of our great market will be felt in every department of productive labor. Under the present system the fruits of industry are appropriated to the wants of idleness; a laborious poor man is taxed for the support of an idle beggar; and the vice of mendacity, no longer considered degrading, infects a considerable portion of our population in large towns. I am persuaded that the sooner a radical reform takes place the better. The evil is contagious, and a prompt extirpation can alone prevent its pernicious extension. The inducement to pauperism may be destroyed by rendering it a greater evil to live by charity than by industry, its mischiefs may be mitigated by diminishing the expenses of our charitable establishments and by adopting a system of coercive labor; and its cause may be removed by preventing intemperance and extravagance and by intellectual, moral and religious cultivation. It is the decree of heaven that our lives should be spent in useful or active employment. "In the sweat of thy face shalt thou eat bread, till thou return unto the ground," was the declaration of the Almighty to our first parent; and a course of blind, indiscriminating, prodigal benevolence defeats its own object, by attempting to counteract the laws of our nature, and the designs of Providence. Charity is an exalted virtue, but it ought to be founded on reason, and regulated by wisdom. While we must consider as worthy of all praise and patronage the religious and moral societies, Sunday, free and charity schools, houses of industry, orphan asylums, saving banks and all other establishments, which prevent or alleviate the evils of pauperism, by inspiring industry, dispensing employment and inculcating

---

altered until after the separation of the colonies from the mother country. Though none of the poor relief orders may be traced to any single enactment of Parliament, it is clear that the early settlers drew largely upon their knowledge of English law and tradition in their administration of public relief." Cumming's Poor Laws of Massachusetts and New York, p. 16.

economy; by improving the mind, cultivating the heart, and elevating the character, we are equally bound to discourage those institutions which furnish the ailment of mendacity, by removing the incentive to labor, and administering to the blandishments of sensuality."[9]

PHILANTHROPY

This leads to the larger question of charity or philanthropy which, as the next section and the thesis proper show, had important bearings on education. The prevailing conception of charity is well illustrated in the free ("free" was, at this time, synonymous with "charity") schools. These were maintained by churches, exclusively, and were restricted to the poor of the denomination—until, in some cases, it was financially profitable to admit others.[10] At best it was a recognition of a group obligation toward the unfortunate members of the group—and the group was usually a religious denomination. In fact, charity (and education was a phase of charitable endeavor) was regarded as a primary duty of the church, and it was the church which administered the system of public relief. Unquestionably this was the course of the main current, but below there was a strong undercurrent. The movement toward secularization was its most general expression, and is discussed later. Its concrete embodiment in this connection is found in the poor-relief law of 1784,[11] and the organization of the Association for the Sick Poor in 1795. By the law of 1784, the offices of the church-warden and the vestryman in the city of New York and in Queens, Richmond and Westchester counties were abolished, and the relief of the poor was made a public function, to be administered not as heretofore by church officers, but by public officers. This is a significant indication of the direction in which things were moving. The name of the "Association for the Relief of the Sick Poor," is not exactly descriptive of its function, for it was educational as well as humanitarian in the general sense. Its constitution restricted its membership to the Society of Friends, but provided that "no relief be afforded to the people

---

[9]Messages from the Governors (1818), v. 2, pp. 914-5.

[10]Cf. Documents in School Controversy as published in Bourne's History of Public School Society, pp. 61-63.

[11]Chap. 35, Laws of 1784.

called Quakers." When the society opened a school in 1801, it was intended for those whose parents belonged to no religious society, and who, from some cause or other, could not be admitted to the charity schools of the city.[12]

As a private matter, philanthropy was sustained by religious sanctions as now, but much more universally then—the personal reward of the charitable in a future life. Or as Cummings rather aptly puts it: "The system of poor relief was founded upon a liberal interpretation of the doctrine that it is more blessed to give than to receive, which mainly regarded the poor and needy merely as a means of grace given by divine wisdom to the end that the elect may have proper exercise for their virtues."[13]

But that misery or indigence was frequently of social origin *and no matter what its origin,* had important social effects, and that the remedy, charity, or whatever you choose to call it, was a vital social problem—a view which Clinton was about to impress upon his generation in a masterly way—had hardly been conceived by the community itself or by any large group in the community—except possibly the Quakers. The proposal that the community was the only power to deal with the problem in a large and comprehensive way, was against the individualistic bent of the people; it was "undemocratic." And yet it is easily demonstrable, were this the place, that such community action is the only possible reconcilation between charity and democracy.

As remarked above, the poor relief law of 1784 was an indication of the direction in which things were moving, i. e., the movement from a religious to a secular view of human affairs. The Free School Society itself offers further indications of this movement. It announced as a "primary object" that in Sunday School as in the Common School, "it will be a primary object, without observing the peculiar forms of any religious society, to inculcate the sublime truths of religion and morality contained in the Holy Scriptures." As usual the religious motive is asserted. This of itself is not noteworthy. But the publications of the society during its first year (1805) are prophetic of the new tendency.

---

[12]Cf. Original name of Public School Society.
[13]Poor Laws of New York, p. 16.

From the address "to the public" we learn that its purpose was not merely moral and religious instruction, but "the common rudiments of learning, essentially requisite for the *due management of the ordinary business of life.*" In its memorial to the Legislature, this new note was sounded more clearly: "The consequences of this neglect of education are ignorance and vice, and all those manifold evils resulting from every species of immorality, by which public hospitals and alm-houses are filled with objects of disease and poverty, and society burthened with taxes for their support." And again: "The rich having ample means for the education of their offspring, it must be apparent that the laboring poor—a class of citizens so evidently useful—have a superior claim to public support."

THE GENERAL MOVEMENT TOWARD SECULARIZATION

But the movement toward secularization was broader than this, and had been gaining impetus steadily during the eighteenth century. It is impossible here to indicate its progress in Europe since the Reformation, nor its course in New York State during the colonial period. Its momentum can be judged by two facts of post-Revolutionary history.

The first, of wider significance, is found in the Constitution of the United States. Section three of article six requires that "no religious test shall ever be required as a qualification to any office or public trust under the United States," and the first clause of the first amendment is: "Congress shall make no law respecting an establishment of religion or prohibiting the free exercise thereof." The other is the Regents legislation. By the Act of May, 1784, the church was permitted no *ex officio* regents and instead there was to be an elective clerical representative who might be a member of any sect. Further, any denomination might establish a professorship in divinity. And, finally, there was to be no religious tests for professors. This applied only to Columbia College, and any prospective colleges organized by the Regents. The legislation of 1787 went even further by providing that there was to be no clerical representation as such on the Board of Regents or the trustees of any college or academy. It was provided with reference to Columbia, for example, that the old charter be "absolutely ratified and confirmed in all respects except . . . . that no persons shall be trustees of the same in virtue of any offices, characters, or description whatever, excepting also such clauses as require the taking of oaths and subscribing the declaration therein mentioned, and which render a person ineligible to the office of President on account of his religious tenets; and prescribe a form of public prayer to be used in the said college." Practically the same provisions were made for the academies.

CHAPTER II

EDUCATIONAL CONDITIONS

INTRODUCTORY

Educationally, things were at a low ebb at the beginning of the nineteenth century. Naturally the upheaval caused by the Revolution was evident in every phase of human activity. Governor George Clinton in his message of January 21, 1784, says: "Neglect of education is among the evils consequent on war—perhaps there is scarce anything more worthy your attention than the revival and encouragement of seminaries of learning; and nothing by which we can satisfactorily express our gratitude to the Supreme Being for his past favors, since piety and virtue are generally the offspring of an enlightened understanding."[1]

Education was very inadequately provided for at the beginning of the century; elementary education more so than either secondary or advanced.[2] There were no public elementary schools, few academies, and only two colleges. There were a few professional schools, but attendance at these was not a necessary passport to the practise of the profession.

The elementary schools so far as they existed were ungraded and housed most unsuitably. More often the elementary school was the living room of some old woman of the neighborhood— the "dame school." Teachers were untrained and were in many cases illiterate. Expert supervision of instruction was probably not dreamed of. Text-books were few and poor. Compulsory school attendance and all the machinery of the present-day educa-

[1]There is no mention of education in the first constitution of the State.

[2]Cf. the following divisions of this chapter "Higher Education," and "Private Schools within New York City." Cf. especially Gov. George Clinton's statement in 1795 given later.

tion were non-existent. So likewise was the provision for defectives and delinquents.

TYPES OF EDUCATION

Common School Education or the Education of the English School[3]

The Buildings. In the Regents Report to the Legislature in 1794, it was pointed out, as already indicated, that common schools were greatly neglected in those parts of the State remote from the academies. However, there were common schools independent of the academies; such schools as, for example, the one kept by Ichabod Crane. These buildings were usually small, one-room, one story frame buildings, "without the slightest attempt at architectural beauty." A detailed description of the school buildings in New Rochelle from 1791-1796, follows:

"The inside of these school houses was of the crudest and cheapest finish. As to the outside, they were small, unpainted shanties, usually located on some surplus angle of the streets or rocky land, unfit for cultivation, thus economizing ground and making these barren spots, where no vegetation could grow, produce the precious fruits of education. The houses were ceiled round with unpainted boards shrunken from their grooves; consequently no ventilators were needed. Their fixtures were extremely rude and simple, consisting for the most part of pine boards nailed up to the sides and ends of the rooms for desks, with sometimes a shelf underneath on which to keep books and slates. They were furnished with seats of long oaken slabs, with legs driven into auger holes at each end, and all of the fixtures and furniture were curiously notched and carved into many fantastic and grotesque images by the busy jack-knives of the mischievous tyros. The school-room was sometimes warmed by a fire in an open fireplace, but mostly by a small cast-iron stove set upon a pile of bricks in the middle of the room."[4]

There is a peculiar inversion of a problem we are dealing with, in connection with the old school house. We are trying to make a social center of the school house. At the beginning of the last

---

[3]Special attention is given to elementary education, because it was in this field that Clinton made his most significant contribution to education and gave most freely of his great ability.

[4]Coutant's Reminiscences. Cf. also Scharf's History of Westchester County, p. 696.

century, the school activity was carried on in the social center.[5] In a description of the old school house in Utica, it is stated that it was "the sanctuary of the fathers of Utica and the seat of learning of their sons, as well as the ordinary place of assembly for secular, as well as sacred purposes."[6]

Such a description is significant for its omissions, as well as its inclusions. There were no blackboards, no charts, no maps, no globes—practically nothing in the way of school apparatus except the ferule. A few steps from the door of the school house you were in the midst of nature in her infinite variety—but nature-study was not a school-study at the time. The arrangement of the room seems to indicate that the class recitation as we know it was not possible, i.e., that the instruction must have been individual. A study of the text-books confirms this inference.

Organization. The common school of the period was frequently the lower school of the academy. It was natural that if the academies were to have any students to pursue the academic studies and in the absence of any other adequate institution, they must themselves give the prospective student his preparatory training. To anticipate somewhat a report that will be given in full later,[7] it may be pointed out that in the sixteen academies reporting to the Regents in 1804, there were 963 students in all. In fourteen of these academies reporting the fact, 480 students were studying reading and writing, 429 students in sixteen academies were studying grammar and arithmetic, while only 213 students in fifteen academies were studying the "dead languages." The conditions are even more striking in 1807. In nineteen academies reporting there were 1,490 students. In eighteen of these academies reporting the fact, 631 students were studying reading and writing, while only 214 in fifteen academies were studying the "dead languages."

Provision for common school education was made also by the ministers in their homes.[8] For example, on March 4, 1801, Rev. Seth Hart advertised that he "was disposed to take 6 or 8 boys to board and lodge in his family and be instructed in reading, writ-

---

[5]Cf. Newburgh also.
[6]Bogg, Pioneers of Utica, p. 92.
[7]On page 39.
[8]Cf. Ondernook's Queen County, p. 91.

ing, arithmetic, geography, English grammar, and the Latin and Greek languages." Sometimes, as in the case of Rev. Matthial Burnet, the minister himself taught the Latin and Greek, and an assistant was engaged "to attend part of every day to instruct (such as may desire it) in writing, vulgar arithmetic and book-keeping."[9]

Beside these types there was in New York City another type—the merely private common school—the teachers of which were not "boarded round," nor aided by the literature fund of the State, and the sessions of which were not held in the public school house. The Goodrich and Ely School in Albany is an academic representative of this class; others are given under the head of private schools. In the New York City directory for 1786, it is announced that Edward Fogarty taught reading, writing, and arithmetic and language if required, from nine to twelve and from two to five o'clock each day in his school at 46 Wall Street. At other times he would "attend a Ladie's Boarding School or families."[10] So likewise John Trent Care taught reading, writing and vocal music in his school. He also taught a morning school from six to eight o'clock for young ladies.[11]

The Teachers. The teachers in such schools were untrained. In the message of 1826, De Witt Clinton wrote: "With full admission of the merits of several who now officiate in that capacity (i.e., of teachers), still it must be conceded that the information of the instructors of our common schools does not extend beyond rudimental education." Along with the facts given in the preceding section, this is a fair statement of the situation. Such a situation is perfectly intelligible, when we remember that in the United States there were no teachers colleges or colleges with pedagogical courses, no normal or training schools, no teachers' institutes, not even the pedagogical departments—a course of lectures on the "Principles of Teaching" in the academies. There were no magazines specially or even incidentally devoted to education. No distinctly pedagogical work had been written or

---

[9]Newspaper: May 17, 1784.
[10]New York City Directory, 1786, p. 139.
[11]*Ibid.*, p. 134.

printed in America, except text-books.[12] However, during the last decade of the eighteenth century, at least one association of teachers was formed: the Society of Associated Teachers, organized in New York City in May, 1794. This society held meetings until 1807 at least. The first institution in America to make actual provision for the training of teachers was the Public School Society, of New York. This work received legislative recognition in 1827. This will be treated in detail later.

The Text-Books. Dr. Francis was a student with Washington Irving in 1797 in a male seminary on John Street, New York.[13] He says, "I remember well the elementary books scattered about, so characteristic of a common English school, at that period the Columbian Orator of Bingham, and Hamilton Moore's Monitor: the School-master's Assistant of Dilworth and the Arithmetic of Pike, with here and there a copy of Dytch's English Dictionary." After commenting on the presence in the school room of ballads on "Commerce," "Freedom," and the like, he proceeds to say: "The leading teacher was ever insisting on the importance of rhetoric, and striving to make everybody a Cicero; he assigned to Irving the heroic lines: 'My voice is still for war,' while I, nearly seven years younger was given for rhetorical display: 'Pity the sorrows of a poor old man.' The Principal stuck earnestly to Dilworth, while the assistant, for his instruction, held to Noah Webster; the slender duodecimo volume of Morse's Geography was in use. There was a special teacher of elocution by the name of Milne." It will be profitable to examine these text-books, actually used in the schools of New York State, to find out somewhat more definitely the method and content of the elementary school education of the period.

The School-Master's Assistant,[14] by Dilworth, was an arithmetic text by a British school-master, used extensively in America before the days of Pike. The twenty-third edition was published in 1786.[15] An accurate notion of the field covered by this work and its character may be secured from its title page:

---

[12]Cf. Christopher Dock's Schul Ordnung. Neef's Sketch of a Plan and Method of Education was published in 1806.

[13]Dr. Francis, In Old New York, p. 3. Also Irving Memorial, 66-68.

[14]Preceding all the editions examined, there is "an Essay on the Education of Youth humbly offered to the consideration of parents."

[15]Copy in Lenox Library, New York.

"The 'School-master's Assistant,' being a compendium of arithmetic, both practical and theoretical in five parts containing:

"1. Arithmetic in whole numbers, wherein all the common rules, having each of them sufficient number of questions with their answers, are methodically and briefly handled.

"2. Vulgar Fractions, wherein several things not commonly met with, are there distinctly treated of and laid down in the most plain and easy manner.

"3. Decimals, in which among other things, are considered the Extraction of Roots; Interest, both simple and compound; annuities; rebate and equation of payments.

"4. A large collection of questions with their answers serving to exercise the foregoing rules, together with a few others, both pleasant and diverting.

"5. Duodecimals, commonly called cross multiplication, wherein that sort of arithmetic is thoroughly considered and rendered very plain and very easy; together with the method of proving all the foregoing operations at once by division of several denominations, without reducing them to the lowest terms mentioned.

"The whole being delivered in a most familiar way of question and answer. . . . ."

Pike's Arithmetic. Pike's famous arithmetic is described on the title pages of various editions as "a new and complete system of arithmetic for the use of citizens of the United States." It was a book of 5½ by 8 inches, consisting of 576 pages and costing $2.50.[16] It was intended to supplant the "School-master's Assistant."

This purpose is avowed indirectly in the preface to the first edition: "but as the United States are now an independent nation it was judged that a system might be calculated more suitable to our meridian than those heretofore published." Another purpose of the text is indicated in this same preface by this statement: "Among the miscellaneous questions, I have given some of a philosophical nature, as well with a view to inspire the pupil with a relish for philosophical studies as to the usefulness of them in the common business of life." This text was not completed in the common school as a list of its contents will show.[17] The preface

---

[16]Advertisement in *Mercantile Advertiser.*

[17]Besides the fundamental processes, duodecimals, the rule of three and "rules for reducing all the coins from Canada to Georgia, also English, Irish and French coins and Spanish dollars each to par"—the usual course of study in arithmetic—there were sections on the following:

to the third edition says that it has been introduced "as a classic into several of our universities."

The defects of this work are indicated in the "publisher's notice" in an abridgment. Two especially are pointed out: the one, want of conformity to the federal notation, and the other, simplicity and attraction to the scholars in a few of the rules. The following paragraph is also found in this notice:

"Some of the old and obsolete rules of tare and trett, etc., have been omitted and the duties of custom house allowance of our own country substituted. Several rules such as Position, Alligation, Permutation, etc., are inserted in this work more for the purpose of gratifying the curiosity and exercising the mind than for their utility in business."

And it is truly remarkable how those subjects which so early were regarded simply as gratifying the curiosity and exercising the mind were continued in the texts until near the end of the century.

Morse's Geographies.[18] Morse prepared on a concentric circle plan, resembling very much the series of language texts prepared by Comenius, a series of four books on geography. The first is a small astronomical and geographical catechism for the use of children under eight years of age. The second, the "Elements of Geography," intended primarily for children from eight to fourteen years old, but "usefully read by those

---

Single and Double Fellowship; Fellowship, Tare and Trett, Involution, Evolution, Arithmetical and Geometrical Progression, Commission, Alligation Medial and Alternate, Position, and Permutation and Combinations. Besides these subjects there were miscellaneous questions on gravity, on screws, and the specific gravity of bodies. In addition there were a series of chronological problems which are utterly unintelligible to the school teacher of to-day. The following is an example:

"To find the Gregorian Epact. Rule—Subtract 11 from the Julian Epact. If the subtraction cannot be made add 30 to the Julian Epact, then subtract, and the remainder will be the Gregorian Epact, if nothing remains the epact is 29.

"Or take 1 from the Golden Number, divide the remainder by 3, if 1 remains add 10 to the dividend which sum will be the epact; if 2 remains add 20 to the dividend, but if nothing remains, the dividend is the epact."

The use of logarithms was also taught, and the plane geometry of the right angle triangle and mensuration in fifty-four articles.

[18]Copies of these texts in various editions may be secured in the Lenox Library, New York. Teachers College has a copy of the eleventh edition of "Geography Made Easy." (1807) The twentieth edition was published in 1819.

of more advanced years." This is the text referred to by Dr.
Francis. "Geography Made Easy" is the third of the series and
is confessedly an abridgment of the American Universal Geography, and is intended for use in the higher classes of the
academies. The final one is the great "American Universal
Geography"—a complete system for the higher classes of the
academies, for colleges, and for private families. The title page
of this indicates the range covered in each of these works. It
reads:

"The First Part treats of astronomical geography and other
useful preliminaries to the study of geography in an enlarged and improved introduction—of the Western or American
continent—of its discovery—its aboriginal inhabitants and
whence they came—its divisions—but more particularly of the
United States of America, generally and individually—of their
situation, dimensions, divisions, rivers, lakes, climate, mountains,
latitude, produce, natural history, commerce, manufacturers, population, character, curiosities, springs, mines and minerals, military
strength, constitutions, islands, history of the war and the succeeding events—with a view of the British, Spanish, French,
Portuguese and other dominions in the continent and in the
West Indies."

The second part gives similar facts for the remainder of the
world.

Dilworth's New Guide to the English Tongue. For the study
of language there were three famous texts: the work respectively
of the author of the "School-master's Assistant," of Caleb Bingham, and of the greatest of all, Noah Webster. Dilworth's text
was used during Noah Webster's school days. Says Webster:
"When I was young, the books used were chiefly Dilworth's
Spelling-book, the Psalter, Testament and Bible. . . . . No
English grammar was generally taught in common schools when
I was young except that of Dilworth's."[19]

Dilworth's text is a "New Guide to the English Tongue," in
five parts, which had reached its forty-sixth edition in 1784.[20]
This was a combination child's prayer-book, language book, reader
and speller. It had forms of prayer for children on several oc-

---

[19]*American Journal of Education*, v. 25, p. 961.
[20]The 1784 edition was used. This copy was secured at the Lenox library.

casions. It set the standard of form and arrangement practically for the nineteenth century. First—that is, after the alphabet—there was a list of monosyllables, those of two letters first, then three and so on. Following that there was a list of polysyllables beginning with those of two syllables and ending with words of six syllables. The third part was a "large and useful table of words that are the same in sound but different in significance." The two remaining parts are indicated accurately in the following quotation from the title page:

"A useful collection of sentences in prose and verse, divine, moral and historical, together with a select number of fables for a better improvement of young beginners.

"A short but comprehensive grammar of the English Tongue, delivered in the most familiar and instructive method of question and answer; necessary for all such persons as have the advantage of an English Education."

Caleb Bingham's Texts. The Bingham books are the "American Preceptor," which was first published in 1789, and which reached its sixty-eighth edition in 1829, and the "Columbian Orator," published in 1799 and designed "as a second part" of the "American Preceptor." The former of these "was a new selection of lessons for reading and speaking designed for the use of schools." In the preface the author says that preference is given to works of American genius; that no place is given to romantic fiction; and that "tales of love have not gained admission." "Nor," says he, in the next paragraph, "is there to be found a word or a sentiment which would raise a blush on the cheek of modesty." The selection is exceedingly miscellaneous. By way of introduction there are the rules for elocution and the select sentences. Among the selections are: Franklin's "The Whistle," J. Q. Adam's "Oration," "George Washington's Resignation," "Mr. Pitt's Speech, 1775," "Brutus and Cassius," an oration of Demosthenes, a speech of St. Paul's, and four quotations from Addison. The "Columbian Orator" is simply a three hundred page second volume.

Webster's Grammatical Institute of the English Language. "In the year 1782," writes Noah Webster, "while the American army was lying on the bank of the Hudson, I kept a classical school in Goshen, Orange County, State of New York. I there compiled elementary books for teaching the English language. The county was then impoverished, intercourse with Great Britain was interrupted, school books were scarce and hardly attainable, and there was no certain prospect of peace."[21]

In that statement is found the origin of the "Grammatical Institute of the English Language, comprising an easy, concise and systematic method of education designed for the use of English schools in America." The "Grammatical Institute" was made up of three parts: a speller, a grammar and a reader. The first edition of each of these was published, respectively, in 1783, 1790, 1792. The design of the "Institute," one reads in the preface to the first part, "is to furnish schools of this country with an easy, accurate and comprehensive system of rules and lessons for teaching the English language." The patriotic and literary purposes are stated definitely in the same preface as follows: "to diffuse uniformity and purity of language in America—to destroy the provincial prejudices that originate in the trifling differences of dialect and produce reciprocal ridicule—to promote the interest of literature and the harmony of the United States."

The title page of the first part of the "Institute," the famous Webster "blue-back," reads as follows: "The American Spelling Book, containing an easy standard of pronunciation, being the first part of a grammatical institute of the English language—to which is added an appendix, containing a moral catechism and a federal catechism."[22] In form and arrangement it is very similar to Dilworth, and frequently in substance. Instead of the different forms of prayer for children it substitutes the moral and the federal catechism. In the speller proper there is some noteworthy changes. The names of all the local places of England, the abbreviation of English titles are omitted and American geographical names and the like substituted. In short, Webster's "blue-back" is practically an American adaptation of Dilworth.[23]

Part two of the "Institute," is the grammar, "a plain and comprehensive grammar," the title page reads. The "Advertisement" informs us as follows: "As this work is designed for general use, the most necessary rules and definitions are given in the

---

[21]Quoted in Scudder, Noah Webster, p. 33.

[22]The 1798 edition was used. It was secured at Teachers College, New York.

[23]It may be said, in passing, that Webster's list of words is more pedagogical.

text by way of question and answer." "The design of this part of the Institute," the preface says more definitely, "is to furnish schools with a collection of rules or general principles of English grammar." The first quarter of the book—twenty-nine pages—is a catechism on the rules of grammar, and exactly the same amount of space is given to false syntax. The remaining fifty-eight pages are given over to many of the finer points of language and to punctuation and grammar.

"An American Selection of Lessons in Reading and Speaking calculated to improve the minds and refine the tastes of youth, and also to instruct them in the geography, history and politics of the United States to which is prefixed rules in elocution and directions for expressing the principal passions of the mind," constitutes the third part of the "Grammatical Institute."[24] The lessons in this book are classified under four headings: Lessons in Reading; Lessons in Speaking; Dialogues; and Poetry. Typical selections under each are: Under the first: Discovery and Settlement of America, "Geography of United States," "Brief History of the Late War"; under the second: Hancock's and Warren's "Orations on the Boston Massacre," "First Petition of Congress to King of Great Britain," Cicero's "Oration against Verres," and "Speech of Caius Marius"; under the third heading: "Brutus and Cassius," "Wolsey and Cromwell," and "Shylock and Tubal"; under the last: Shakespeare's "The World Compared to a Stage," and quotations from Pope.

The Content of a Common School Education. The school session was short—very short; attendance was intermittent; teachers were frequently incompetent; the benefits of a class recitation were not realized and consequently the acquirements of the scholars were limited. After attendance at school for a few winters, pupils gained a tolerable proficiency in reading, writing, and ciphering through the "rule of three." Under the conditions this was no mean accomplishment. But those who secured what was called at that time a "good English education," gained much more. Arithmetic included besides arithmetic proper, a smattering of elementary science, inventional geometry, and the mathematical side of astronomy. The reading material included valuable but most uninteresting supplementary geographical, historical

[24]The 1792 (Hartford) edition was used.

and political information. Geography, itself, included history, an elementary discussion of astronomy, civil government, and much miscellaneous information on a wide range of topics. Geography was, like reading, a general information subject. There was, during this period, tremendous emphasis on what Bingham calls the "ornamental and useful art of eloquence." This is a case of a clear response of the curriculum to the social demands of the time.

The Method. While much might be said in favor of the curriculum, especially as contrasted with the isolated character of modern courses of study, little or nothing can be said in favor of the method. For in the first place, it is utterly mechanical. The method of solution of the chronological problem given by Pike and quoted above is one indication of this mechanical process. The progress of the spelling book on the mere basis of length of words or number of syllables, is so much more evidence of this. The catechetical method—the method of Dilworth, of Morse, and of Webster—is the expression, from another viewpoint, of this mechanical character. There was no searching of the mind on the part of the pupils; no attempt to formulate problems; no expression of individual opinion; no contributions from the various members of the class—none of the advantages of the modern recitation. The pupils came up to the teacher; the teacher took the book, asked the appropriate question to which the pupil gave as dutifully and as mechanically the set reply. It need only be named to be perceived that this mechanical, catechetical, individual method placed the emphasis on Memory, which means ultimately, "words, words, words."

The Spirit. One thing apart from the method and content of the education strikes you forcibly while reflecting upon these texts: it is that there is here consciously the attempt to embody the new spirit of American life—call it what you will, a new patriotism, democracy or Americanism. Here is conscious, mental revolt—as conscious as the political one. Pike thought that since the United States had become an independent nation, a system (of arithmetic) might be calculated more suitable to our meridian than those heretofore published. Likewise, Bingham announces in his preface that preference is to be given to the publications of American genius. But in Webster this spirit is strongest.[25] The preceding text-books are condemned because they are not specially designed for American schools. And it is declared—such heretical doctrine—that the Revolutionary orations are not inferior in any respect to the orations of Cicero and Demosthenes. This result, the new democratic spirit, extends in Webster's case even further: it extends to the Latin domination of the English language as opposed to the language of the people. The sentences on this subject in the preface to part two of the "Institute," are emphatic and virile. The Lindley Murray domination would never have been, had Webster gained the day, but here tradition and the opposing forces were too strong for him.

ACADEMIES—A CLASSICAL EDUCATION

The following account deals with typical aspects of the various academies: the buildings, subjects of studies and rates of tuition, the library and apparatus; the text-books; the teachers; and the students.

The Erasmus Hall Academy, a neat, two-story frame building, consisting of four large halls, thirty-four by twenty-two feet, for the use of students, and twelve lesser rooms for the teacher and boarders, was built in 1786. It was incorporated by the Regents on November 17, 1787—the same day as the Clinton Academy at Easthampton. The rates of tuition were from two to five dollars per quarter. The exact prices for the various subjects or group of subjects are not given. But we can be sure they were not different from those of the Clinton Academy. There, the rates of tuition per quarter were $1.50 for reading and writing; $2.50 for English grammar and ciphering; and $5.00 each for mathematics and book-keeping; the dead languages; logic, rhetoric, and

---

[25]In the Preface to Webster's American Selections, are the following statements:

"But none of these (a list given, including the "Preceptor"), however judicious the selection, is calculated particularly for American schools. The essays respect distant nations or ages, or contain general ideas of morality."

"In the choice of pieces I have been specially attentive to the political interest of America. I consider it as a capital fault in all our schools that the books generally used contain subjects wholly uninteresting to our youth, while the writings that marked the Revolution, which are not inferior in any respect to the orations of Cicero and Demosthenes, and which are calculated to impress interesting truths upon young minds, lie neglected and forgotten."

composition; moral philosophy; natural philosophy; or the French language.[26]

Erasmus Hall had a library of 650 volumes. This was the largest number in any academy in New York State at the time; i.e., of those reporting to the Regents in 1804-05. The Oyster Bay Academy had no library;[27] Columbus Academy at Kinderhook had but 17 volumes;[28] Lansingburgh but 42;[29] while Farmer's Hall at Goshen had 556.[30] Erasmus Hall had, too, practically a complete outfit of the apparatus used in the academy of the day; a set of elegant globes, an orrery, an air pump, a telescope, an electrical machine, a thermometer, a barometer, a Hadley's quadrant, a theodolite and chain, two prisms, a magnet, drawing instruments, maps, etc.[31] The only other piece of apparatus mentioned in the reports of the other academies is a case of surveying instruments, at Union Hall, Jamaica.[32]

The texts used in these academies are given in the following list taken from a minute of the trustees of the Oyster Bay Academy:[33]

English: 1. The Monitor—to be read daily as the last lesson; 2. Webster's Grammar—to be read or repeated by memory; 3. The Testament or Bible—to be read by inferior scholars and once a day by all.

Latin: 1. Ross', Ruddiman's, or John Holmes' Grammar; 2. Colloquia Corderii, Erasmus, Selectae Veteris, Selectae Profanis, Nepos, Aesop's Fables, Florus, Mair's Introduction, Cæsar, Virgil, Cicero's Orations and De Oratore, Horace.

Greek: Moore's Grammar, Testament, Lucian's Dialogues, The Cyropædia, Longius, the Iliad.

Rhetoric: Blair's Belles Letters.

Geography: Guthrie's or Solomon's Grammar.

Mathematics: Stone's Euclid, Martin's Trigonometry, or Warden's Mathematics.

An interesting sidelight is thrown upon the teaching and teachers of the academies in the special message sent to the Legislature by Governor Lewis in February, 1805.[34] The subject of

---

[26]Report to Regents, 1805. Hough, p. 414. This report and the others mentioned below are to be found summarized *in* Hough, pp. 412-421.
[27]Report, 1805.
[28]Report, 1804.
[29]Report, 1805.
[30]Report, 1805.
[31]Report, 1804.
[32]Report, 1805.
[33]Newspaper reprint: Ondernook's Queens County, p. 80.
[34]Messages from the Governors, vol. 1, p. 557.

this message is the establishment and distribution of an "adequate, permanent and certain" school fund. The Governor doubts the wisdom of permitting academies to participate in such distribution. His opinions are the result of reflections carried on for twenty years, while "I had the honor," he says, "of being a trustee of Columbia College."

His first reason is the difficulty of keeping them (the academies) supplied with unexceptionable teachers. He observes that the academies that have come under his observation have been for months at a time without a teacher. This was due to the fact that many of the men who taught in the academies were just from college and were using teaching as a stepping-stone to the recognized professions. "A suspension of academic instruction is the consequence, and before a successor can be procured, the students are frequently dispersed." Then add to this first fact, these others: that each teacher introduces a new system of education, and that the systems in the different academies are likewise diverse, and consequently "there is an almost insurmountable difficulty of pursuing with effect a collegiate course"—and it will be understood why the Governor thought academies should not participate in a general fund.

Young women were apparently admitted to the academies, for the Lansingburgh Academy in a report to the Regents in January 1805, says that the "average board for males, exclusive of washing, was about $2.00 per week, and for females, $1.50." It is unlikely in the light of the subsequent history, especially of the work of Mrs. Emma Willard, that the young women studied the substantial or serious part of the curriculum. Possibly some clue may be found in the advertisement of the Union Hall Academy at Jamaica in the *New York Journal*,[35] "a room is devoted to the instruction of young ladies in the refinements of the needle."

Fashionable Education[36]

A prevailing type of education, i.e., fashionable education, is keenly and accurately characterized by Timothy Dwight, thus:

---

[35]June 3, 1796.

[36]In a dialogue in Bingham's Columbian Orator, the preceptor soliloquizes thus:

"I am heartily sick of this modern mode of education. Nothing but trash will suit the taste of people of this day. I am perplexed beyond all

"The end proposed by the parents is to make their children objects of admiration. . . . . That I have not mistaken the end may be easily proved by a single resort to any genteel company. To such company the children of the family are regularly introduced, and the praise of the guests are ministered to them as regularly as the dinner or tea is served up. . . . .

"The means of effectuating this darling object are the communication of, what are called, accomplishments. The children are solicitously taught music, dancing, embroidery, ease, confidence, graceful manners, etc., etc. To these may be added what is called reading, travelling. . . . ."[37]

This form of education was embodied in special institutions. The directories and newspapers of 1786 indicate that there were the following main types. There were riding schools for the improvement of gentlemen desirous of acquiring the art of riding with grace and elegance. A typical school gave lessons four days a week, from six to eight in the morning, and from four to six in the evening for ten dollars.[38] There were many musical schools, both for instrumental and for vocal music. Some advertised simply as singing schools, some as schools for vocal music and others as schools which taught the "harpischord, German flute and clarinet."[39] Dancing schools were numerous. "The days of attendance," one advertisement reads, "will be on Monday, Wednesday and Friday, from nine to twelve in the morning for young ladies, and on the same days for gentlemen, from six to nine in the evening."[40] Another school announces the same hours for men, but takes the ladies in the afternoon from two to five. Fencing schools were also very numerous.[41] Other schools contributed an intellectual veneer, such as the French schools, the purpose of which was to give a mastery of French; and the

---

endurance with these frequent solicitations of parents, to give their children graceful airs, polite accomplishment, and a smattering of what they call the fine arts; while nothing is said about teaching them the substantial branches of literature. If they can but dance a little, flute a little, make a handsome bow and courtesy, that is sufficient to make them famous in this *enlightened* age. . . . . For my part, I am convinced that, if I had been a dancing-master, music-master, stage player or mountebank, I should have been more respected and much better supported than I am at present," p. 185.

[37]Dwight's Travels, v. 3, pp. 512-13.
[38]New York City Directory, 1786, p. 182.
[39]*Ibid.*, p. 126.
[40]*Ibid.*, p. 168.
[41]*Ibid.*, pp. 163 and 251, for example.

schools where young gentlemen were taught useful and polite literature.[42]

The arrangement of hours for these various kinds of education for the different sexes is significant. For the young gentlemen, hours are either very early in the morning or very late in the afternoon or in the evening, so that the main part of the day is given over to more substantial studies or to the occupations of life. The arrangement of hours for the young ladies would seem to indicate that these special forms of education were their main occupation. In the main, so far as they were admitted to the schools, giving presumably the more intellectual work, it was only early in the morning, during the noon recess, or in the evening, that is, at odd times. This will appear more evident in the subdivision headed "Private Schools." These, so far as the young ladies were concerned, combined this fashionable education with more solid studies, or, at least, presumed to do so.

Private Schools

In addition to the fashionable schools there were several private schools; the main type may be indicated in the following advertisements. The first though in New Jersey apparently attracted the genteel young women of New York. It is quoted here because the advertisement appeared in a New York paper, and gives the curriculum of the Young Ladies Seminary in full:

BETHESDA SELECT BOARDING SCHOOL.

PATERSON, NEW JERSEY.

The *House* lately occupied by a *Hotel*.

By the desire and approbation of several respectable families, Mrs. Philip has altered her plan and has taken that well-known house at Paterson. Her terms are $451 per annum, which includes Board, Spelling, Reading, Grammar, Writing, Arithmetic, Geography, the use of Globes, Plain Work, Marking, Darning, Embroidery, Clock Work, Point Work, Filigree raised and flat, Paper Work, Tambour, Muslin Work of every description, making Artificial Flowers, etc. Several young ladies of genteel family are already engaged, and she has room for many more. She desires to acknowledge with gratitude the favors she has received from many families in New York, and hopes still to meet their patronage.

Further particulars may be known respecting the school by inquiring of Mrs. Howe at her Music Warehouse on Pearl Street.

The health, morals and behavior of the young ladies will be particularly

[42]*Ibid.*, pp. 163, 178, 110 and 251.

attended to. They will not be allowed to walk out without sufficient attendance. [43]

In Mrs. M. Scott's school at the corner of Smith and Duke streets, young ladies received practically the same instruction as in the foregoing; the same attention was paid to "forming the manners and improving the morals of those tender minds committed to her care." It was also announced that "for those who desire to be taught writing, a proper master will attend three days in the week."[44]

Another, a shorter advertisement, indicates definitely the subjects taught, the provision for the education of girls and for the evening school.

James Main's Academy, No. 10 Gold Street, for the English, French, Latin and Greek Languages, Writing, Accounting, Mathematics, Geography, is again open for the reception of his pupils.

An Evening Class from 6 to 8.

Tuition for young ladies between hours of 12 and 2. [45]

Still another advertisement seems to indicate that some of these private schools had a narrower curriculum: "Mr. Coffey has removed his grammar school to No. 21 Smith street, where he instructs youth in the Greek and Latin languages." The advertisement goes on to say that "if the number of his students exceeds twenty-five, Mr. Coffey engages himself to engage an assistant."[46]

THE EDUCATIONAL MOVEMENT—1787-1800[47]

The Regents' Interest in Common Schools

The committee appointed by the Board of Regents, January 13, 1787, have given in their report of February 16, 1787, an excellent statement of the situation, with reference to the common schools and its only solution. They say:

"But before your committee conclude, they feel themselves bound in faithfulness to add that the erecting of public schools for teaching reading, writing, and arithmetic is an object of very great importance, which ought not to be left to the discretion of private men, but ought to be promoted by public authority. Of so much

[43]*The Commercial Advertiser*, Aug. 20, 1799.

[44]*Ibid.*, Nov. 5, 1799.

[45]New York City Directory, 1786, p. 166.

[46]*Ibid.*, 1786, p. 166.

[47]Cf. Andrew Draper's speech before N. Y. State Teachers' Association (1890), on the "Origin and Development of the New York Common School System."

knowledge no citizen ought to be destitute, and yet it is a reflection as true as it is painful that but too many of our youth are brought up in utter ignorance. This is a reproach under which we have long labored unmarred by the example of our neighbors who not leaving the education of their children to chance, have widely diffused throughout their State a public provision for such instruction.

"Your committee are sensible that the Regents are invested with no funds of which they have the disposal, but they nevertheless conceive it to be their duty to bring the subject in view before the honorable, the Legislature, who alone can provide a remedy."

The Regents made two other significant statements on this subject in their reports to the Legislature in 1793 and 1794, respectively. In the first of these the Regents urged upon the Legislature, because of the general social results that would follow, the desirability of establishing schools where children would be taught "the lower branches of education, such as reading their native language with propriety, and so much of writing and arithmetic as to enable them when they come forward in active life, to transact with accuracy and dispatch the business arising from their daily intercourse with each other."[48] How this is to be accomplished is left to the Legislature. Such a recommendation would have been pointless, if there existed to any general extent these schools for the common branches[49] and judging from the rapidity of settlement and the character of the settlers, conditions would become worse—were actually becoming so. The condition is admirably and emphatically pointed out in the 1794 recommendation.

"After another year's experience and observation, we beg leave to solicit the attention of the Legislature to the establishment of the schools for the common branches of education—an object of acknowledged importance and extensive utility. Institutions of this description, so well adapted for the diffusion of that kind of knowledge which is essential to the support and continuance of a republican government, are greatly neglected, *especially in those parts of our country (i. e., State) remote from the academies. The numerous infant settlements annually forming in our State chiefly composed of families in very indigent circumstances and placed in the most unfavorable situations for instruction appear to call for legislative aid in behalf of their offspring.*"[50]

[48]*Senate Journal*, 1793, p. 93.
[49]Cf. below: "Educational conditions in various places."
[50]*Senate Journal*, 1794, p. 16.

It was not until the next year (1795), that there was any legislative response to these recommendations, and perhaps even then, the Legislature would not have responded but for the repeated and emphatic co-operation of Governor George Clinton. Or it would be more in accord with the facts to say that the result was brought about through the reinforcement of the Governor's vigorous recommendations, by the emphatic statements and suggestions of the Regents.

The First Statute Relating to Elementary Schools

In the meantime there was passed (1791) the first statute relating to an elementary school in New York State.[51] The preamble reads:

"Whereas, the magistrates, town-officers, and other inhabitants of the town of Clermont in the county of Columbia have by their petition represented to the Legislature that there are moneys in the hands of the overseers of the poor of said town arising from the excise, and from fines which are not wanted for relief of the poor and prayed that so much of the said money as shall remain in the hands of the overseers on the first of April next, and *shall not then be wanted for the support of the poor of said town, may be by law appropriated to the purpose of building a school house and maintaining a school-master in the same town,* and that Robert R. Livingston . . . . may be authorized to put such a law in force."

There you have the system at its best. Heretofore, apparently, education of the poor was not regarded as a town function nor even a phase of poor relief. In this instance it was to be provided for, from the money not wanted for the relief of the poor—and, moreover, to use this money, appeal had to be made to the Legislature. Of course, the fundamental conception is that education is a private matter and a phase of charitable endeavor.

The Law of 1795

The law of 1795 was the first general statute relating to elementary schools—and the only one passed during the eighteenth century. It was "An act for the encouragement of schools." In addition to establishing the district system, it appropriated fifty thousand dollars a year for five years "for the purpose of en-

---

[51]Chap. 41, Laws of 1791.
Chap. 75, Laws of 1795, passed April 9.

couraging and maintaining schools in the several cities and towns
of this State, in which the children of the inhabitants residing in
this State shall be instructed in the English language, or be taught
English grammar, arithmetic, mathematics, and such other
branches of knowledge as are most useful and necessary to complete a good vocation." The act required the town to raise
as much as it received from the State. Energetic efforts were
made in 1800 and thereafter to secure a continuance or renewal
of the act, but all failed until the Common School Fund was provided for in 1813.

The Breakdown of the Law of 1795 in the Long Island Towns

If the Long Island towns are typical of the whole State, the
system organized under the Act of 1795 broke down completely.[52]

At the town meeting in Huntington, to take that for illustration,
on April 4, 1797, four commissioners of schools were appointed
among persons to transact public business. Similar provision was
made in April, 1798, but no provision was made in 1799 and 1800,
for the election of these officers. No reference to schools is found
after 1800 until 1813, when three school commissioners were
elected and it was "voted that the town raise, by tax, as much
money as is granted to said town by law, from the Common School
Fund." At a special town meeting on December 23, 1813, six
inspectors of common schools were elected, and a similar election
was held in 1814. Thereafter commissioners and inspectors were
elected annually during our period.

Huntington is typical of the other Long Island towns; in Easthampton, Southampton, Babylon, and Brookhaven, the same provision for education was made from 1795 to 1800; then there is
absolutely no mention until 1813 of any similar provision or continuance of the old provisions.[52] In that year the distribution of
the Common School Fund began and these towns complied with
the law.

It may be well to note that in Easthampton in 1796, and again in
1797, 1798, 1799, and 1800 the town clerk, supervisors and as-
sessors were chosen commissioners of schools. And at the town
meeting of April 3, 1798, it was "voted that the trustees be im-
powered to repair the school house."

---

[52]The town records of these towns.

EDUCATIONAL CONDITIONS IN VARIOUS PLACES

In New York City. The later Public School Society was incorporated by an act passed April 9, 1805. It was an act incorporating the "society for the establishment of a free school in the city of New York for the education of such poor children as do not belong to or are not provided for by any religious society." The name of this society clearly indicates several things. It indicates that there was no such thing as a public school in our sense—open to the public free of expense—for then these children could have been provided for. It indicates that there were no charity schools open to all poor children. It indicates, too, that there were several schools by the various religious denominations, and open only to the poor of the denomination. It intimates that these charity schools did not provide for all the poor members of the denomination, for the act provided for "such poor children as are not provided for by any regular religious society." It is also intimated that the richer children were provided for by other means, either by tutor at home, or in private schools.

In an 1805 Directory,[53] it is stated that church schools were supported by the Dutch Reformed, Episcopal, Presbyterian, Methodist and Roman Catholic denominations. The Roman Catholic school had the largest number in attendance; one hundred. The school, in connection with the New York Orphan Asylum (the first of its kind established), was not organized until 1806. Sunday Schools were also used to give secular instruction. There was also a special school to give colored children the elements of an education. This school was conducted by the Manumission Society. It was opened in 1787 in Cliff Street and soon numbered one hundred children. Several other schools were organized by the Society later.

In Jones' Directory for 1805-06, there are given fifteen thousand names. Those who have any connection with education whatever are grouped under the heading: "Learned professions and public officers." A careful examination of this list shows that there are eighty-six men classed as teachers simply and thirty-three women. Of the women, twelve were widows and five were

[53]Longworth's New York Register, 1805-06, p. 76.

married. In addition two men are given as "teacher and book-seller," and as "teacher and captain of the city watch," respective-ly.

All the other persons given are indicated as teachers of special subjects; though in the list is found a "junior" and an "assistant" teacher. Of these special teachers there are 3 teachers of language, 1 of mathematics, 2 of French, 1 of French and music, 1 of French and English. 1 of German, 1 of music, and 1 merely a teacher in academy. There is also listed 2 writing masters, 1 teacher of needlework, 1 teacher of navigation, 1 philosophical lecturer, 1 moral and philosophical lecturer, and 1 professor of music.

Examination of the list reveals also the number of certain types of schools. There are given the names of twelve academies or seminaries for young ladies; two boarding schools and one Episcopal academy. The academies were conducted, in the largest number of cases, by married women. There is listed also two drawing academies, one academy of painting and one mercantile academy.

In Albany. Albany was the other large city of the State at this time. In the *Gazette* of 1789, a writer says: "At that period (seven or eight years ago) a competent English teacher was scarcely to be found. We have now an academy which flourishes under the direction of Mr. Merchant." "In 1785 Elihu Goodrich and John Ely opened a school. . . . They taught Greek and Latin for 40s a quarter; grammar, arithmetic and writing for 30s; reading and spelling for 20s. The hours of study were from 6 to 8, and from 9 to 12 in the forenoon, and from 2 to 5 and from 6 to 8 in the afternoon."[54]

In the *Albany Register* of November 1, 1799, there is the ad-vertisement of the Trinity School. This school, so the advertise-ment reads, prepared its pupils for the "University, Navy, Army, or Counting House." In an earlier advertisement printed during the same year, the terms of tuition are given as follows: "The Greek and Latin languages, History, Geography, and the other branches requisite for completing a good classical education, four dollars. Mathematics, three dollars. Spelling, reading, writing

[54]Munsell's Annals of Albany, v. 2, pp. 201-2.

and arithmetic, two and a half dollars, but with modern history, geography, or grammar, three dollars." The advertisement concludes with the usual remark: "Diligent attention shall be paid to the improvement of the pupils in good morals and useful learning. Public examination will be held twice a year."[55]

Albany had its schools for giving fashionable or polite education. Mr. Danglebut, for example, announces in the *Albany Register* in an advertisement dated September 20, that he will open on October first, his dancing school, "where he will teach music on the Forte Piano, Violin, German Flute, Flageolette and Clarinet."[56] A Mr. Carpenter announces in the same paper the opening of a dancing school. "He flatters himself that by his manner of teaching, his scholars will soon acquire those graceful deportments and easy manners, which are so highly useful in society."[57] Mr. Carpenter also announces that in compliance with certain solicitations he will open an academy of the French language, provided he secures enough students, and that he will continue to give instruction in private families as usual.[58]

In Hudson. There was in Hudson as early as 1785 provision for the three types of education regarded as essential in those days: the elementary, the academic and the fashionable or polite. Seventeen hundred and eighty-five is the year of the incorporation of Hudson. At that time there was one school house, a small frame building standing on the country road near the river. Apparently the proprietors regarded this school house as unsatisfactory, for on April 19 of the same year they voted:

" . . . . that a lot 50 x 120 on Diamond Street would be granted to any person or persons, who would build a school house not less than 40 feet by 24, such persons not to receive more than nine per cent. on the cost of the building for the use of it and to have the power to sell it to the corporation at large for their own use whenever they had opportunity so to do and that it should continue to be used for a school house for every description and denomination of people then settled or which should thereafter settle."[59]

[55]*Albany Register*, Sept. 6, 1799.
[56]Cf. issue of Nov. 1, 1799.
[57]Issue of April 29, 1800.
[58]Issue of April 8, 1800.
[59]Ms. Reprinted in Miller's Historical Sketches of Hudson, p. 12.

Beside being used for the main purpose we find in the proprietor's minutes that a Joseph Marshall designed opening a school in the Diamond Street school house, from 5 to 7 o'clock P. M. each day, for the instruction of misses in writing, ciphering, composition, English grammar, and geography.[60]

The Hudson *Gazette* contained two interesting advertisements during the same year. The one is the advertisement of Ambrose Liverpool. He advertised that he would open a seminary "where he would teach all the English branches, also at convenient times the principles of several musical instruments, and that he had several dozen strong English beer to dispose of."[61] The other is the advertisement of M. Robardet, from Connecticut, who advertised that he would open a class for instruction in the polite accomplishments of dancing after the most approved method. Scholars varying in age from seven to fifty are received.

In a newspaper of Nov. 26, 1805, one reads, "a school building was erected by the charitable contributions of the benevolent for the benefit of neglected and helpless female children; and a family of twenty-three gathered under the care of a discreet governess were daily instructed in reading, writing and plain work, and in the strict observance of every Christian and moral duty."[62] In August, 1810, there was being considered the project to establish a free school on the plan of Joseph Lancaster. As yet it is believed there were no public schools in the city. The society of mechanics had a number of years previously erected a building in Chapel Street, called Mechanics' Hall, and maintained a school out of their funds, but it is presumed that its benefits were confined chiefly to the children of mechanics.[63]

In Newburg. In the letters patent of Dec. 18, 1719, the town of Newburg was known as Quassing. In the letters patent of March 26, 1752, it was given its present name. These letters vested the lands in two persons named in the document in trust "for the proper use, benefit and behalf of a minister of the church of England as by law established to have the cure of souls of the aforesaid tract of 2,190 acres of land and of a schoolmaster to

---

[60]*Ibid.*, p. 3.
[61]*Ibid.*, p. 62.
[62]Munsell's Annals of Albany, v. 4, p. 332.
[63]*Ibid.*, v. 1, p. 74.

teach and instruct the children of the aforesaid inhabitants and their successors forever, and to no other use whatever." From the "Account Book of the Glebe," it is known that this school was continuously in existence from 1760 to the Revolution. From the same source it appears that Richard King was the teacher from 1782 to 1790.[64]

In 1790 the following agreement was made with the Reverend Mr. Sperin:

(The Trustees) "Agreed that the Reverend George H. Sperin shall be entitled to receive the whole of the rents and benefits arising from the Glebe lands, while he continues to officiate as minister, and teaching the inhabitants of the German patent on the following terms, *viz.*: Reading, Writing, Arithmetic, Geography, History and English Grammar at 12 shillings per quarter; Reading, Writing and Arithmetic at 8 shillings per quarter.

"Provided always that no children incapable of studying the above branches shall be admitted or received into the school.

"And should a poor child come properly recommended as such, he shall be received into the English school gratis.

"And if a youth of strong natural ability of the like description offer, he shall be received into the Classical school, also gratis.

"Provided also that should the rents and privileges of the Glebe hereafter become more valuable, that then, in such cases, the terms of teaching the children living in the patent shall be reduced in such manner as to be equivalent to said advantages, so far as may relate towards supporting of a school and as the trustees shall deem proper."[65]

During the same year the Reverend Mr. Sperin advertised in the *Goshen Repository,* wherein he "informs the public that he proposes opening an academy for the instruction of youth in the Greek and Latin languages and the different other branches of literature, when a sufficient number of pupils shall offer themselves. . . . Boarding, washing, and lodging at 20 pounds per year (or $1 a week), and 5 pounds for tuition." It is significant that those who wished to encourage the enterprise were to send their names to the minister or "to Isaac Belknap and Cadwallader Calden, Trustees of the Glebe Lands at Newburg."[66] In an advertisement in the *New York Journal and Patriotic Register*

---

[64]p. 33.
[65]Minutes of the Trustees. Printed in Ruttenher's History of the Town of Newburgh, p. 245.
[66]*Goshen Repository*, July 13, 1790.

dated "Newburg, August 6, 1791," Mr. Sperin informs the public
that he has "engaged as an assistant in his academy at Newburg, a
young man eminent for his mathematical ability, and that in addition to the Greek, Latin and English languages—logic, rhetoric,
history, geography, etc., the following branches will be taught:
Vulgar and decimal arithmetic, book-keeping, mensuration, navigation, gauging, surveying, dealing, geometry, astronomy and
algebra at his usual price of two pounds per annum."[67]

In 1803 there was passed "An act to alter and amend the charter
of the Glebe land in the German patent in the village of Newburg."
It provided that the "moneys arising from the annual income of the
Glebe shall forever thereafter be appropriated solely to the support of schools on the said Glebe."[68] Regarding the distribution
of the money, it is provided that the trustees of the Glebe shall
give two hundred dollars to the trustees of Newburg Academy,
"who shall apply the said sum of two hundred dollars solely to the
use of schools taught in the academy," and that the remainder
shall be paid "to the trustees of other schools which are or may
hereafter be established on the Glebe."

In the Mohawk and Black River Counties. The Journal of Rev.
John Taylor, narrating his doings on a "Mission through the Mohawk and Black River counties in the year 1802,"[69] gives some insight into the educational conditions in that region. In Amsterdam there is no school mentioned, but he observes that among the
Dutch who constituted one fourth of the inhabitants, a considerable portion can neither read nor write. At Whitesborough, four
miles from Utica, which contains no church, he notes "in this town
or rather parish, is an academy, which is in a flourishing state.
A Mr. Porter, an excellent character and a preacher, is preceptor.
They have one usher and about sixty scholars."[70] At Floyd,
which is eleven miles north of Utica, and which contains eight
hundred inhabitants, he writes: "I then visited a school of about
thirty children, catechised them, gave advice and prayed with
them. On inquiry I found they had but few school books and no
catechisms."[71] On August 23, 1802, he visited a school at Camden

---

[67]Cf. issue of *New York Journal* for Sept. 14, 1791.
[68]Chap. CX, Laws of 1803.
[69]p. 112.
[70]Extending from July 20 to Oct. 12, 1802.
[71]p. 114.

and gave the "instructress" five catechisms. In the next five towns visited no mention is made of schools. On Sept. 8, he visited a school of twenty-five children in Champion, which had an excellent "instructress." There are seventy families in the town. In the next thirteen towns visited there is no mention made of schools. In Northampton he visits a school, and on his return no mention is made of schools in the eighteen towns he visited. However, at Williamston he visited the College, which had ninety scholars, a president and four tutors and two elegant buildings. At Clinton, he saw Clinton Academy from the distance.

HIGHER EDUCATION

History of the Regents. "There were no efficient educational institutions. A few private and parish schools, a few academies, King's College defunct—such was the condition of education in 1783,"[72] i.e., before the organization of the Regents. We have had Governor George Clinton's statement of the situation and his recommendation for the revival and encouragement of seminaries of learning.

The status of higher education in New York State is intimately connected with the history of the Regents. To state, therefore, the conditions of higher education it will be necessary to trace the history of the Board of Regents.

On May 1, 1784, there was passed, "An act for granting certain privileges to the College heretofore called King's College, for altering the name and charter thereof and erecting an university within the State."[73] This was in part in response to Governor Clinton's suggestion, and the petition of the governors of King's College— most of whom were members of the State government—dated March 24, 1784, submitting the charter for revision and correction to the Legislature and requesting its aid.

The first section of the act vested all the rights, privileges and immunities heretofore granted to King's College in the Regents of the University of the State of New York, "who are hereby erected into a corporation or a body corporate and politic." This section named certain State officers, the mayors of New York and Albany, two men from each county as Regents of the Univer-

---

[72]Sherwood's University of the State of New York, p. 48.
[73]Chap. 51, Laws of 1784.

sity and provided for the election of the representatives of the clergy of the respective religious denominations. Section two provided for the filling of vacancies. Section three, four and five, provided for the management of Columbia. Other sections provided for the founding of academies, the amount of estates, real and personal, that may be held, for the endowment of a professorship of divinity, for the granting by the University of the degrees that may be conferred by all or any of the Universities of Europe, and for changing the name of the college from King's to Columbia. An amendatory act was passed November 26, 1784,[74] which named thirty-three new Regents and provided that a quorum should consist of nine, including the Chancellor. However, both these acts were repealed by the last section of the act of April 13, 1787.[75]

The twenty-two sections of this act may be divided into four general subdivisions. The first seven sections provide for the incorporation of the University, its management, organization, powers, and duties. The next four sections (8-11), provide for the organization and control of Columbia College. The following eight sections (12-19) provide for the incorporation, organization, and control of the academies. The last three sections (20-22) are general and miscellaneous in character.

It is well at this point to give in more detail the provisions for incorporation of academies and colleges. Section seven enacts: "That any citizen or citizens or bodies corporate, within this State being minded to found a College at any place within the same, he or they shall, in writing, make known to the Regents the place where, the plan on which, the funds with which it is intended to found and provide for the same, and who are proposed for the first Trustees; and in case the said Regents shall approve thereof, then they shall declare their approbation by an instrument under the common seal and allow a convenient time for completing the same. . . . If satisfactory, then the Regents shall forthwith incorporate the Trustees, who shall have perpetual succession, and enjoy all the corporate rights and privileges enjoyed by Columbia College, hereinafter mentioned." Section twelve enacts that the

[74]Chap. 15, Laws of 1784.
[75]Chap. 82, Laws of 1787.

Regents have somewhat similar power in the incorporation of academies.

This Regents legislation passed so soon after the Treaty of Paris, was an indication that the government was going to exercise vigorously its control over education—at least in the field of secondary and higher education. This was regarded at the time as the proper field for state activity and this limitation of the sphere of state activity furnished the basis for the establishment of two distinct organizations for the public control and administration of education. The Legislature kept control of elementary education in its own hands until in 1812 it transferred its executive and some of its legislative functions not, as might have been expected, to the Regents of the University, but to the newly created officer, the Superintendent of Common Schools.

But practically from the beginning the Legislature delegated its power over secondary and higher education to a private corporation—the Regents of the University—a private corporation which however was created by the Legislature, its membership maintained by the Legislature and accountable to the Legislature. It was practically a State Bureau of Education—a central organ of administration and control.

Academic Education. Up to the beginning of the nineteenth century, nineteen academies were incorporated. Those incorporated during the last decade were Washington and Montgomery in 1791; the academy of Dutchess County and Union Hill in 1792; Hamilton, Oneida, Refugees and Schenectady, in 1793; Johnstown and Oxford in 1794; Kingston and Canandaigua in 1795; Cherry Valley, Lansingsburgh and Ostego in 1796; and Columbia in 1797. The following table indicates in a general way, the situation with reference to the incorporated academies :[76]

---

[76]Hough, p. 421.

STUDIES TAUGHT	1804		1805		1806		1807	
	No. of Acad.	No. of Students.	No. of Acad.	No. of Students.	No. of Acad.	No. of Students.	No. of Acad.	No. of Students.
Reading and Writing..	14	480	10	205	10	208	18	631
English, Gram. and Arith.	16	429	10	228	10	312	19	649
Math., Bookkeeping, etc..	12	123	7	36	7	51	15	134
Dead Languages	15	213	9	184	10	130	15	214
Logic, Rhet., Comp., etc.	6	101	4	48	4	38	17	97
Moral Philosophy, etc..	—	—	1	1	2	14	3	22
Natural Philosophy	—	—	1	1	3	14	4	36
French Language	4	38	1	1	—	—	4	16
Total number of students.	16	963	11	652	10	671	19	1490
FUNDS.								
Value of Academy lot and building	17	37948	11	27650	9	22350	19	50150
Value of other real estate.	6	3837	4	8400	6	6453	7	16250
Value of personal estate.	8	4556	5	4400	6	5292	8	9006
Value of Library and Apparatus	14	5771						
ANNUAL INCOME								
From funds	7	626	3	210	6	594		487
From tuition	12	7036	6	3878	9	5398		9745

Teachers' salaries in Farmer's Hall, Union Hall, Clinton and Columbia Academies are not reported, the teachers receiving tuition money for pay.

Collegiate Education. The acts (1784) organizing the Regents, provided for the revival of Columbia College. DeWitt Clinton was the first matriculated student of Columbia College.[77] He received the bachelor's degree in 1786 and the master's in 1789.

The act of 1787 gave Columbia its own Board of Trustees who, on May 21, elected Willian S. Johnson, LL.D., President. There were then—Nov. 12, 1787—three professors in Arts, three in Medicine, but none in Law or Divinity. "An extra Professor of German was employed, but without fixed salary."[78]

---

[77]Cf. "De Witt Clinton and Columbia"—*Columbia University Quarterly,* Sept. 1909.

[78]Hough, p. 121.

In 1792,[79] the college received a grant of £7,900; £1,500 for a library, £200 for chemical apparatus, £1,200 for a wall to support grounds and £5,000 for a hall and wing to building. Their next grant was after the opening of the century (1801), when Columbia shared with Union a land grant in the northern part of the State.[80]

After many unsuccessful attempts to found a college at Schenectady, beginning with the proposed Clinton College in 1779, a college was incorporated on February 25, 1795—Union College.[81] The financial condition of the college was reported in 1798 to be as follows:

```
Given by Trustees of the Town .............................$20301.60
Given for House and Lot ...................................  5712.50
House and Lot for President ...............................  3500.00
Lot on which new College is to be built ...................  3250.00
Philosophical and Mathematical apparatus and Library ......  2516.00
Cash raised for apparatus and Library but not expended ....  1234.00
                                                           ----------
                                                            $36514.10
```

In addition to this property the College owned 1,640 acres of improved lands. The faculty consisted of a president, a professor of Natural Philosophy and Astronomy, a professor of Mathematics and one tutor. The Legislature before this had made the following appropriations:

```
Act of April 9, 1705, for books and apparatus ................$3750.00[82]
Act of April 11, 1796, for building...........................10000.00[83]
Act of March 30, 1797, for salaries two years ................ 1500.00[84]
```

Libraries. Now for a few words as to the chief suplementary means of education: libraries. During the colonial period there were six attempts to establish an institutional library in New York, exclusive of the purely commercial circulating libraries—these last principally owned by booksellers. These attempts were the Trinity Parish Library, 1698; the Sharpe Collection (1713-15), which never attained an independent existence; the Corporation Library

---

[79]Chap. 69, Laws of 1792.
[80]Chap. 82, Laws of 1801.
[81]Chap. 92, Laws of 1795.
[82]Chap. 76, Laws of 1795.
[83]Chap. 57, Laws of 1796.
[84]Chap. 65, Laws of 1797.

(1754) ; the Library of King's College (1757) ; and the Union Library Society (1771).

All of these were prostrated by the war. But two of these later became significant in the intellectual life of the city and State, but only after they began anew.[85]

Professional Education. Professional education was not more advanced than elementary. So far as there was any, it was carried on by an apprentice system. Judging from the absence of special schools, and the failure of the medical and law school established in connection with Columbia, it may fairly be said that the people had not yet in any adequate degree felt the necessity for a scientific preparation for professional men.

Divinity: Apparently the ordinary way of preparing for the ministry was by placing oneself under the instruction of a regularly ordained minister and later be examined by a Board of Ministers. In 1784 the Dutch Reformed Church discontinued the above practice and indicated two of its members to do the work.

However, in 1784, Dr. John Livingston, pastor of the Collegiate Church of New York City, was elected by the synod to be professor of divinity in the church at large. Until 1810 when Dr. Livingston became head of Rutgers College and its professor of divinity, he taught the students gratuitously. About ninety men were licensed during this period. It will be observed that this is essentially the empirical way, and it is not, strictly speaking, professional preparation. The colleges, of course, prepared for the ministry. Divinity was taught in Columbia and in the College of New Jersey, Yale, Harvard, and William and Mary. So also were Greek and Hebrew.

Law: There was but one attempt to establish a law school in New York in the eighteenth century (1797), and that was a failure. This was the attempt made by James Kent in connection with Columbia. Mr. Kent delivered but a single course of lectures, and it was not until sixty years later that a department of law authorized to grant degrees was established at Co-

---

[85]For a full and detailed discussion of this subject see Keep's, The New York Society Library, to which the writer is indebted for the facts in the preceding paragraph.

lumbia. It may be remarked here that Chancellor Kent was an intimate friend of Clinton's, and also that the subject of professional education for lawyers did not receive any consideration from Clinton. This is the more surprising when we remember that Clinton was himself a lawyer, and one of no mean attainments.

Medicine: The first and only attempt in New York to establish a medical school before the beginning of the nineteenth century—in fact, the first of the academic institutions to provide medical instruction, was the organization in 1766, of a medical department in connection with King's (Columbia) College. The faculty consisted of six. In 1770 two students who had previously received the degree of Bachelor (B. M.) were granted the degree of Doctor of Medicine (M. D.)—the first conferred in the country.[86]

It will be seen that professional education before the nineteenth century and well into the nineteenth century was not theoretical and practical, but merely empirical. The medical schools were the offices of the practising physicians; the law schools were the offices of the practising lawyers; the theological seminaries were largely the studies of the minister's houses.

The Financial Situation

The conception that money spent on education and the like for the removal of adverse social conditions and the improvement of others, was not really a government expenditure, but an investment—an investment that would yield a manifold return in the form of a worthier citizenship—or, if you choose, a citizenship with greater tax-paying capacity, has not, as yet, gained currency. Without some such conception, in such adverse conditions as prevailed, the amount of money involved in the organization of a state system in any thorough-going way, would have made such a project utterly disheartening. The attitude of the people toward rate bills later—and the difficulty of collecting them, indicates that even a half century later, the financial problem was far from solution. The failure of the legislation of 1795 was an early indication of this. It was a gigantic proposition which Clinton and his colleagues had undertaken. The creation of a permanent state

---

[86]Cf. Davis contributions to the History of Medical Education and Medical Institutions in the United States of America, 1776, 1876, p. 20.

school fund was a master stroke in hastening the day of the socially supported school system. The Lancasterian system was a vital factor in this problem. Both are discussed in detail later.

CONCLUSION—THE GENERAL SITUATION

George Clinton clearly saw the situation and comments on it keenly in his speech to the Legislature of January 3, 1795. He says:

"While it is evident that the general establishment and liberal endowment of academies are highly to be commended and are attended with the most beneficial consequences; yet it cannot be denied that they are principally conferred on the children of the opulent and that a great proportion of the community is excluded from their immediate advantage; the establishment of the common school throughout the State is happily calculated to remedy this inconvenience and will therefore re-engage your early and decided consideration."

While it is true that in the academies, in a number of instances, the elementary subjects were taught, it is also true that academies were encouraged almost to the extent that elementary schools were neglected.

Reflection on the preceding statement will show that so far as formal education is concerned, the grade most adequately provided for was the higher education in the academies and colleges; the grade of education most needed was the elementary. A pressing need in all schools was well-trained teachers; but it was most pressing in elementary schools. An education for girls beyond sewing and reading, and co-ordinate with that of boys was not seriously considered by the eighteenth century.

And what as to the governmental relation to education? The wide powers of the Regents—who were practically a State Bureau of Education—is a striking instance of this with reference to secondary and higher education. But what a contrast the field of elementary and special forms of education presents! Apart from the temporary expedient of an annual appropriation for five years to the local communities, which were required to raise an equal amount, there is absolute silence. No instance whatever of state encouragement, aid, support, control, or administration of the professional training of teachers; of various supplementary means of education, such as libraries; of the education of women in academies or elsewhere; of professional training of doctors or lawyers; of technical education; of the education of delinquents or defectives. Nor had the State, itself nor exercising its power, delegated it to the inferior administrative units.

It seems rather surprising that the conditions of American life did not force these needs and problems to the foreground for formulation, at least, if not for solution. It is not so surprising after all when we remember that there were, as already explained, other problems more immediately significant to the people of New York. It was left for DeWitt Clinton in the first quarter of the nineteenth century to formulate the problems in detail—though it must be admitted others had stated them in general terms—and to strive heroically and persistently for their solution.[87]

---

[87]De Witt Clinton, the second son of James Clinton and Mary De Witt; born at Little Britain, March 2, 1769; educated at Kingston Academy,1782-1784, and Columbia College, 1784-1786; received from Columbia the B. A. in 1784, the M. A. in 1786, and the LL. D. in 1824 and from Queen's College the LL. D. in 1812; studied law in the office of Samuel Jones 1786-1789, and was admitted to the Bar 1789; Secretary to Governor George Clinton 1789-1795; married Marie Franklin (died 1818) a Quaker, 1795, and had four sons and three daughters; Secretary, Board of Regents, 1794-1797; Regent of the University, 1808-1828; member of the Assembly 1797-1798; member of the State Senate 1798-1801, 1803-1811; Lieutenant-Governor, 1811-1813; United States Senator 1801-1803; Mayor of New York City 1803-1807, 1809-1810, 1811-1815; Canal Commissioner 1809-1824 (removed); candidate for President 1812 (defeated); Governor 1817-1822, 1825-1828; married Catherine Jones 1824; died at Albany, February 11, 1828.

PART II

EDUCATIONAL VIEWS OF DE WITT CLINTON
AND THEIR SIGNIFICANCE

CHAPTER III

EDUCATIONAL VIEWS OF DE WITT CLINTON

THE FUNDAMENTAL PROPOSITION—THE SOCIOLOGICAL CONCEPTION

In this chapter is given a statement of Clinton's educational views as revealed in his speeches and messages to the Legislature as the Chief Executive of New York State. That a lay person should, in the early nineteenth century, have held educational views of such insight and such breadth, is truly remarkable. With Clinton, however, the fundamental conception was not original. It may be found in the utterances of a number of the American statesmen of the time. It may be found in the writings of Jefferson and Madison. For example, its most popular expression is found in Washington's "Farewell Address": "Promote then as an object of primary importance, institutions for the general diffusion of knowledge. In proportion as the structure of government gives force to public opinion, it is essential that public opinion be enlightened." However, in no other writer of the period, with the possible exception of Jefferson, is there so decisive, clear, and convincing a statement of the underlying sociological conception, as in De Witt Clinton. In no other writer, without exception, are the implications of this conception so clearly and fully conceived and so forcefully expressed.

De Witt Clinton's fundamental conception of education is the current sociological one. It regards education as the salvation of mankind, as the means through which society will set about consciously to improve itself, as the absolutely indispensable foundation to democracy. Its implications as conceived and expressed by Clinton, relate to the extent of education, its method, its aspects, its institutional organization, its officers, and its support. Education should extend to all classes. It should not be merely literary or academic, but should include the vocational as well; both the professional and the technical, as well as the trade. It should have a scientific basis. It should be given by every possible type of educational institution, the less formal: the literary, philosophical and historical societies, as well as the more formal institutions: the elementary school, academies, and colleges. It should be in the hands of informed and specially trained teachers. In all its forms it should be aided by society acting in its corporate political capacity, and at least in its earliest stages, the elementary school, should be so supported.

De Witt Clinton has in several of his messages to the Legislature stated his fundamental thesis. In 1825 he wrote:

"A republican government is certainly most congenial with the nature, most propitious to the welfare and most conducive to the dignity of our species. Man becomes degraded in proportion as he loses the right of self-government. Every effort ought, therefore, to be made to fortify our free institutions; and the great bulwark of security is to be found in education; the culture of the heart and the head; the diffusion of knowledge, piety and morality. A virtuous and enlightened man can never submit to degradation; and a virtuous and enlightened people will never breathe in an atmosphere of slavery. *Upon education we must therefore rely for the purity, the preservation and the perpetuation of republican government.*"[1]

In 1826, he wrote: "I consider the system of our common schools as the palladium of our freedom for no reasonable apprehension can be entertained of its subversion, as long as the great body of the people are enlightened by education."[2] In the January, 1820 speech, he said: "The stability and duration of republican government depends upon the ascendency of knowledge and virtue. The mind duly enlightened and the heart properly cultivated can never submit to the dominion of anarchy and depotism."[3] In the 1826 message there is found this excellent statement of the proposition which is here

---

[1] Messages from the Governors, v. 3, p. 60. See *infra* 156.
[2] V. 3, p. 117.
[3] V. 2, p. 1018.

used by way of summary. "The first duty of government and the surest evidence of good government is the encouragement of education. A general diffusion of knowledge is the precursor and protector of republican institutions, and in it we must confide as the conservative power of the state that will watch over our liberties and guard them against fraud, intrigue, corruption and violence."[4]

Such is the main proposition It may be briefly restated thus, with some of its implications. The people are the "supreme and sovereign power of the community, . . . the source of all legitimate government." It is essential, therefore, that they be enlightened. As a matter of self-protection, and self-perpetuation the state must assume the duty and the responsibility of securing this general enlightenment. It must encourage every necessary means to secure this great end and, if necessary, create new ones. It must support liberally—or, to use Clinton's own words— "munificently," all such means. It must see to it that these means reach every class—yes, every member, irrespective of race, color, sex or condition in life.

In such a statement emphasis is not placed on the results of education in terms of individual culture or discipline. It is nearly always on the protection, preservation, and perpetuation of the republican form of government.

Its Realization

The Lancasterian System. The State undertaking so tremendous a task, naturally sought for the system which would accomplish its great purpose most expeditiously and with the least expense. Clinton believed that such a means was the so-called Lancasterian system. The ideal of this system was a thousand pupils to a teacher—an ideal which was realized by Joseph Lancaster himself in his London school. The actual teaching was done by monitors.

Reference to this system is found in the messages of 1818, November, 1820, and in 1822. The reference in 1818 is selected for quotation:

"Having participated in the first establishment of the Lancasterian system in this country, having carefully observed its prog-

---

[4] V. 3, p. 114.

ress, and witnessed its benefits, I can confidently recommend it as an invaluable improvement which by a wonderful combination of *economy in expense and rapidity of instruction* has created a new era in education; and I am desirous that all our common schools should be supplied with teachers of this description. As this system operates with the same efficacy in education that *labor-saving machinery* does in the useful arts, it will be readily perceived that it is peculiarly adapted to this country."[5]

The Training of Teachers. Clinton was not afraid to follow his argument whithersoever it led. He saw clearly that if education was of such transcendent importance to the state it could not, to accomplish its mission, be left in the hands of incompetence— to jacks-of-all-trades and masters of none. In the speech of 1820, he said: "The education of youth is an important trust, and an honorable vocation, but it is often committed to unskillful hands. Liberal encouragement ought unquestionably to be dispensed for increasing the number of competent instructors."[6] But the argument is stated in full in the message of 1826:

"Ten years of the life of a child may now be spent in a common school. In two years the elements of instruction may be acquired and the remaining eight years must now be spent in repetition of idleness, unless the teachers of the common schools are competent to instruct in the higher branches of knowledge. The outlines of geography, algebra, mineralogy, agriculture, chemistry, mechanical philosophy, surveying, geometry, astronomy, political economy and ethics might be communicated by able preceptors without essential interference with the calls of domestic industry.

"The vocation of the teacher in his influence on the characters and destinies of the rising and all future generations has either not been fully understood or duly estimated. It is or ought to be ranked among the learned professions. With the full admission of the merits of several who now officiate in that capacity, still it must be conceded that the information of many of the instructors of the common school does not extend beyond rudimental education—that our expanding population requires constant access to their numbers; it is necessary that some new plan

---

[5]V. 2, p. 903.
[6]V. 2, p. 1049.

for obtaining able teachers be devised. I, therefore, recommend a seminary for the education of teachers in the monitorial system of instruction, and in those useful branches which are proper to engraft on elementary attainments. A compliance with this recommendation will have a benign influence on individual happiness and social prosperity."[7]

He follows his argument still further and now makes bold to recommend what the twentieth century has not yet accomplished—a central high school in each county. He says in 1827, in language somewhat similar to that of the message of 1826:

"Too many (teachers) are destitute of the requisite qualifications and perhaps no inconsiderable number are unable to teach beyond rudimental instruction. Perhaps one-fourth of our population is annually instructed in our common schools and ought the mind and the morals of the rising and perhaps the destinies of all future generations to be entrusted to the *guardianship of incompetence?* The scale of instruction must be elevated, the standard of education ought to be raised, and a central school on the monitorial plan ought to be established in each county for the education of teachers and as exemplars for other momentous purposes connected with the improvement of the human mind."[8]

The recommendation of his last message (1828), indicates how this desirable object may be obtained. He says:

"In the meantime I consider it my duty to recommend a law authorizing the supervisor of each county to raise a sum not exceeding two thousand dollars provided that the same sum is subscribed by individuals for the erection of a suitable edifice for a monitorial high school in the county town. I can conceive of no reasonable objection to the adoption of a measure so well calculated to raise the character of our school masters and to double the power of our artizans by giving them a scientific education."[9]

Supervision. Clinton recognized that supervision was a factor in the effectiveness of the school system. In 1826 he made the unusual suggestion:

"I consider the system of our common schools as the palladium of our freedom, for no reasonable apprehension can be enter-

---

[7] V. 3, pp. 115-16.
[8] V. 3, p. 159.
[9] V. 3, pp. 212-13.

tained of its subversion, as long as the great body of the people are enlightened by education. To increase the funds, to extend the benefits, and to remedy the defects of this excellent system, is worthy of your most deliberate attention. The officer who now so ably presides over that department is prevented by his other official duties from visiting our schools in person, nor is he indeed clothed with this power. A visitatorial authority for the purpose of detecting abuses in the application of funds, of examining into the modes and plans of instruction and of suggesting improvements, would unquestionably be attended with the most propitious results."

Its Extent

He now follows his argument in another direction—the persons who are to profit by this education. It is part of this sociological conception of education that education shall be universal—truly universal; that it shall reach all classes and members of society; the male and the female; the white, and the black, and the red; the dumb, the blind; the man young in crime and, if possible, the hardened criminal.

Women. The higher education of women was, at the beginning of the nineteenth century, a novel proposition; but Clinton thoroughly believed in it and urged it upon an unwilling generation insistently and forcefully. In 1819 Clinton said: "Beyond initiatory instruction, the education of the female sex is utterly excluded from the contemplation of our laws."[10] In January, 1820, after noting that the Waterford Academy for female education incorporated at the last session, had already attained to great usefulness and prosperity, he proceeds to say: "As this is the first attempt ever made in this country to promote the education of the female sex by the patronage of government; as our first and best impressions are derived from material affection; and as the female character is inseparably connected with happiness at home, and respectability abroad, I trust that you will not be deterred by common-place ridicule from extending your munificence to this meritorious institution."[11]

Indians and Africans. Just as Clinton drew no sex line in education, so he drew no color line. "In attending to the general

---

[10]V. 2, p. 972.
[11]V. 2, p. 1018.

interest of the community," he said in his speech of January, 1820, "let us not overlook the concerns of two unfortunate races of men, who will be forever insulated from the great body of people, by uncontrollable circumstances, and who ought to receive our benevolence and sympathy. I refer to the Indian and African population."[12] Then, with reference to the Indians, so long as they continue amongst us, he recommends that a board of commissioners be appointed, selected from the religious societies who have interested themselves in the welfare of the Indians. This board shall have power, "to investigate their situation and wants, to diffuse among them education, agriculture, morality and religion, and to recommend to the Legislature such measures as shall be most conducive to the attainment of these desirable objects."[13]

And with reference to the African population a similar recommendation is made: "It is due, however, to justice to say that the establishment of schools and churches for their benefit, under the auspices of benevolent men, has had a benign influence in the improvement of their minds and morals; and it is therefore believed that the benevolence of the State will never be withheld from the encouragement of such laudable undertakings."[14]

Deaf and Dumb. In the speech of January, 1820, and immediately preceding the last recommendations, there is to be found the following statement:

"Among the numerous and interesting objects which have experienced the benevolence of individuals and the countenance of government, it is pleasing to observe that the interests of the dumb and the insane have not been overlooked; two unfortunate descriptions of our fellow creatures shut out from the blessings of social communion and entitled to our deepest sympathy."[15] The annual grant of ten thousand dollars to the governors of the New York Hospital, for an asylum for lunatics, on the Island of New York, is commended, as the judicious direction of the fund by its benevolent administrators. So the New York Institution for the Instruction of the Deaf and Dumb, is approved as having "de-

---

[12]V. 2, p. 975.
[13]V. 2, p. 977.
[14]V. 2, p. 979.
[15]V. 2, p. 974.

served well of the friends of humanity," and he cherishes, "the fullest confidence that you (the Legislature) will take this interesting establishment under your especial protection, and that your munificence will only be exceeded by its merits."[16] One way Clinton suggests of supplying its deficiencies is by taking a liberal portion of the school fund applicable to the city of New York. It is significant that a part of the general school fund is selected for the education of this special class.

Criminals. The criminal class was of special concern to Clinton, as would be expected of one holding Clinton's views. And were Clinton living to-day, there would be no one more thoroughly interested and more actively engaged in our modern system of reform schools, children's courts, patrol system, and other similar developments of the modern sociological movement. The question of the New York House of Refuge and the penitentiary system occupies a large amount of space in the messages. It is treated in the speeches of 1819, January, 1820, November, 1820, 1822, and in the message of 1825.

In 1825, in urging upon the Legislature the necessity of being liberal in the support of education, Clinton points with pride "to one fact derived from past experience." It is: "Of the many thousands who have been instructed in our free schools in the city of New York, *there is not a single instance known of anyone having been convicted of crime.*"[17] Apparently the fundamental proposition is supported by experience.

In 1818, Clinton pointed out that the existing system was a failure. In 1819, he made the following vigorous statement: "The state of our penitentiaries requires your serious consideration and must excite your sincere regret. As the only legitimate object of punishment is to prevent crime, by reforming the offender, by incapacitating him from perpetrating future mischief, or by deterring the others by the infliction; and, as none of these consequences has resulted, the failure must be imputed to the system, its defective arrangement or improper administration. As it has succeeded in other places, and is strongly recommended by the voice of reason, as well as humanity, the fault must be as-

16V. 2, p. 974.
17V. 2, p. 61.

cribed to other causes than the system itself.   In order to reform an offender he must be placed beyond the influence of bad advice and example, his mind and his passion must be disciplined by intellectual, moral and religious instruction; and he must be subjected to privations, to labor and solitude; and in order that his punishment may have effect on the conduct of others, it is equally necessary that it should be certain, and that its realities should be unquestionable.   On the present plan there is no classification of age or crime.   Each apartment is calculated for about eighteen persons.   All descriptions of convicts are crowded together without distinction—the young and the old—the healthy and the unhealthy—the novice and the adept in crime; and here the hardened offender boasts of his vices, unfolds his expedients, and completely eradicates every remaining impression of rectitude.   Such is the perversity of human nature, that a man destitute of virtue will be vain of his vices, and as a spirit of proselytism prevails among the wicked as well as the good, our penitentiaries become schools of turpitude, in which profligacy is inculcated in its most odious forms, and in all its terrible enormities."[18]

What use to make of the pardoning power, troubled Clinton sorely—though in the recommendations of January, 1820, he saw a way out.   Two paragraphs after the preceding in the speech of 1819, we read: "In consequence of the crowded state of the prisons, the executive is reduced to this dilemma, either to exercise the pardoning power to a pernicious extent, or to witness the destruction of the whole penitentiary system.   He is also frequently deceived by misrepresentations; and pardons are sometimes granted to the worst on the recommendations of the best men of the community, who, in listening to their sympathy, lose sight of their patriotism, and who submit themselves to the influence of a sickly and fastidious humanity, *which confines its views to the offender, and does not perceive in his punishment, the establishment of general security.*"[19]

In the speech of January, 1820, Clinton makes what is probably his most important contribution to the subject.   It may be well first to state the recommendations of 1819.   "Each offender should have a separate dormitory.   And, as in the daytime the

---

[18]V. 2, p. 981.
[19]V. 2, p. 982.

prisoners would be employed in labor and under the eye of the keepers, prevented from speaking to each other, and be in the night time, in a state of insulation, punishment would be appalling, and cleanliness, order and regularity would predominate; and as no conspiracies could be formed, no riots or insurrections would occur, and no military guard would be required."[20]   In 1820, after expressing his gratification at the arrangement for solitary cells and separate dormitories in the state prison at Auburn, and commenting on the fact that in no country in the world are fewer crimes committed, he proceeds to recommend "a moral classification of criminals with distinctive appellations and accommodations according to their grade of guilt.   And if the pardoning power be confined to the best of the proposed divisions, a powerful appeal will be made to the hopes and fears, the enjoyments and privations of the prisoners, and a continual incentive to reformation will be in full operation."[21]   In November, 1820, he recommended a paid board rather than the present arrangement, for responsibility could then be placed.[22]

A summary of his recommendations is made in the message of 1822.   He says: "The end of punishment is the prevention of crime by the infliction of pain and the operation of fear; and if in exercising this salutary influence on society, it can at the same time restore the guilty to virtue, it will be entitled to additional credit.   Our present system may be improved in a moral classification of offenders, in the introduction of solitary imprisonment, in the establishment of a diet adapted to the nature of the offense and the character of the criminal, and in a division of prisons, appropriating one for the reception of minor offenders, and the purposes of productive labor, and personal reformation; and the other to severe and inexorable punishment where society should not afford its comforts and where the pardoning power should never reach."[23]

The striking thing in the preceding statement is the distinctly advanced view of punishment—far in advance of his time—that it should be educative if possible.   While Clinton is impatient with the "sickly and fastidious humanity, which confines its views to

---

[20] V. 2, p. 982.
[21] V. 2, p. 1015.
[22] V. 2, p. 1051.
[23] V. 2, p. 1108.

the offender and does not perceive in his punishment the establishment of general security," still, on the other hand, he was searching for a system which would reclaim the offender and make him
a useful member of society. In his earlier messages—those just
quoted from—such a system was merely hoped for rather than
conceived as probable. The proposed moral classification of
criminals with its less severe regimen for the novice and the
person young in crime; with some of the comforts of life, productive labor, the opportunity for personal reformation and the
hope of an abbreviated sentence through executive clemency, was
a step in the direction which Clinton wished to go further and
more decisively, but he did not feel sure of his ground. One can
readily understand, then, Clinton's enthusiastic and whole-souled
approval of the House of Refuge for the reformation of juvenile
delinquents, a practical embodiment of his views.

Juvenile Delinquents. In the message of 1825, the House of
Refuge in the city of New York is first mentioned.[24] In the
message of 1826, an extended appeal is made in favor of it. "The
best penitentiary system which has ever been devised by the
wit and established by the benevolence of man, is in all probability the House of Refuge in the city of New York, for the reformation of juvenile delinquents. It takes cognizance of vice in its
embryo state and redeems from ruin and sends forth for usefulness, those depraved and unfortunate youths who are sometimes in a derelict state, sometimes without subsistence, and at all
times without friends to guide them in the path of virtue. The
tendency of this noble charity is preventive, as well as remedial;
and during the short period of its existence, its salutary power has
been felt and acknowledged in the haunts of vice and in the
diminution of our criminal proceedings. I cannot recommend
its further encouragement in language too emphatic; and I do believe, if this asylum were extended so as to comprehend juvenile
delinquents from all parts of the state, that the same preserving,
reclaiming, and reforming effects would be correspondingly experienced."[25] The appeal is successful, and in 1827, there is the
statement that the grant for the extension and support, in the city
of New York, of the House of Refuge for juvenile delinquents

---

[24] V. 3, pp. 82-83.
[25] V. 3, pp. 130-31.

has been faithfully and beneficially applied.   "A separate and accommodating building has been erected for females, and schools on the monitorial plan have been successfully established. The institution now contains one hundred and thirty-one males and thirty females, who have been rescued from the most abject debasement. . . . .   It must be considered a noble, as well as successful experience in favor of humanity."[26]

Its Institutional Organization

Following his argument in still another direction we find Clinton supporting every variety of educational society—educational in the broader, as well as in the narrower sense.   If education is of such tremendous importance to society, society acting in its corporate political capacity should freely and liberally encourage and support every means of extending it.   However, the indiscriminate encouragement and patronage of these societies, was not a part of Clinton's program.   The steward had to render an account of his stewardship in terms of social service.   In the message of 1825, Clinton writes:

"While our primary schools cannot be too numerous, our highest seminaries ought to be very limited in number.   The creation of a college imposes the duty of endowing it.   We have now four colleges for literary and scientific instruction and two for medical education.   They are all under the superintendence of highly gifted and enlightened men, and are eminently entitled to your liberal patronage.   But until the government shall see fit to augment the funds of existing institutions to the full extent of their wants, I am persuaded that there ought to be no increase; and not even then unless peremptorily required by the exigencies of education.   Perhaps indeed in a case of so much importance, the authority of the Regents of the University ought to be only recommendatory and the incorporating power exclusively vested in the Legislature, as a more safe depository than a single body, as the source from which munificent endowments must emanate, and as most comfortable to the spirit, if not the letter of the Constitution."[27]

The cause of the literary, scientific, philosophical, and historical

---

[26]V. 3, pp. 162-63.
[27]V. 3, p. 61.

societies is urged upon the Legislature in practically every message
and speech. In the speech of 1818, Clinton said: "There
is an intimate and immutable alliance between their advance-
ment (the societies noted above) and the prosperity of the
State."[28] The same reason is given in more detail and much
more significantly in the message of 1827. After urging the
claim of the common school—a cause "consecrated by religion
and enjoined by patriotism"—he continues: "Nor let us be regard-
less of the ample encouragement of the higher institutions devoted to literature and science. Independent of their intrinsic
merits and their diffusive and enduring benefits, in reference to
their appropriate objects, they have in a special manner a most
auspicious influence on all subordinate institutions. *They give
to society men of improved and enlarged minds, who, feeling the
importance of information in their own experience, will naturally
cherish an ardent desire to extend its blessings.* Science de-
lights in expansion, as well as in concentration, and after flourishing within the precincts of academies and universities will spread
itself over the land enlightening society and ameliorating the condition of men. The more elevated the tree of knowledge, the more
expanded its branches, and the greater will be the trunk and the
deeper its roots."[29]

Among the institutions which Clinton specially noted apart
from the House of Refuge, the Orphan Asylum, the Institution
for the Instruction of the Deaf and Dumb, the Lunatic Asylum,
for their distinctly social service, and as worthy of the generous
and munificent support of government, were Columbia, Union,
and Hamilton Colleges, the College of Physicians and Surgeons,
the New York Historical Society, the New York Institution, and
the Mechanic and Scientific Institute of New York. In 1826 he
adds the general recommendation—"and all other establishments
connected with the interests of education, the exaltation of literature and science, and the improvement of the human mind."[30]

This sociological conception regards education simply as the
means of a more thorough and widespread dissemination of all
knowledge. It resembles somewhat the pansophic idea of

[28] V. 2, p. 906.
[29] V. 3, pp. 160-61.
[30] V. 3, p. 118.

Comenius and Bacon, in the early seventeenth century—though it does not attempt to formulate all knowledge—only here there is a more conscious and more insistent emphasis on the production of certain desirable social ends.

This is the idea underlying the recommendations in connection with the institutions noted above, and it underlies several recommendations which follow. This is only the fundamental proposition stated in other terms. In 1825, Clinton wrote: "In furtherance of this invaluable system (the common schools), I recommend the distribution of useful books."[31] In 1827, he makes this significant recommendation: "Small and suitable collections of books and maps attached to our common schools (and periodical examinations to test the proficiency of the schools and the merits of the teachers), are worthy your attention when it is understood that objects of this description enter into the very formation of our characters, control our destinies through life, and protect the freedom, and advance the glory of our country."[32]

Its Scope

Enrichment of Common School Curriculum. This conception of education—securing desirable social results by the diffusion of knowledge—is further illustrated in his recommendations in connection with medical, technical, military, and agricultural education. It will be noticed from these headings that there is no reliance on the three R's as such, nor on the merely formal side of knowledge. The striking statement of 1826 naturally comes to mind that with competent instructors, "the outlines of geography, algebra, mineralogy, agriculture, chemistry, mechanical philosophy, surveying, geometry, astronomy, political economy, and ethics might be communicated . . . . without essential interference with the calls of domestic industry."[33] The proposed central school of the New York Public School Society, would teach "natural philosophy, mercantile arithmetic, book-keeping, and the outlines of natural science."[34] These statements would be much more significant, however, if we knew just what Clinton meant

---

[31]V. 3, p. 61.
[32]V. 3, p. 160.
[33]V. 3, p. 116.
[34]V. 3, pp. 159-60.

by practical mathematics, mercantile arithmetic, etc. This last school he "cannot recommend too emphatically to public patronage and general imitation."

Medical. With reference to medical education, he says: "The appropriations to medical education do not exceed sixty thousand dollars, a sum by no means commensurate with the object. Every well-educated physician becomes not only a conservator of health, but a missionary of science. *Wherever he establishes himself, he will convey and communicate useful knowledge.* Two hundred of our youth annually, dispersed over the country, instructed in medical knowledge and its cognate sciences, will, in the course of a few years, effect an augmentation in the state of general information, equally honorable and beneficial, to the community. And no measure can be more conducive to the prosperity of our medical institutions, to the respectability of the profession, and to the preservation of the public health, than a law rendering an attendance upon lectures in the university, an indispensable passport to medical practice."[35]

Military. After commenting in the 1818 speech, on the fact that war will continue because it is deeply planted in the constitution of human nature, he suggests that essential improvements may be made in the promotion of military instruction. In 1819, he said: "Fully persuaded that you justly appreciate this bulwark of national safety, and this palladium of free states, I consider it unnecessary to press the importance of its encouragement. If the physical force of the state were properly instructed in the military art, it would form an impregnable defense of the country, and I do not despair to see the accomplishment of this desirable object by the establishment of military schools and by the extension of beneficial immunities."[36] In November, 1820, Clinton said: "A laudable provision for the distribution of elementary books in the military art has been confined to the infantry. The other departments of our military force are anxious to enjoy similar benefits."[37]

Agricultural. On the subject of agricultural education, his program, completely outlined, is given in his first message (1818):

---

[35]V. 2, p. 905.
[36]V. 2, p. 979.
[37]V. 2, p. 1050.

"And it has not been sufficiently understood that agriculture is a science, as well as an art; that it demands the labor of the mind, as well as of the hands; and that its successful cultivation is intimately allied with the most profound investigations of philosophy, and the most elaborate exertions of the human mind. If not the exclusive duty, it is certainly the peculiar province of the state governments to superintend and advance the interest of agriculture. To this end, it is advisable to constitute a board composed of the most experienced and best informed agriculturalists and to render it their duty to diffuse agricultural knowledge; to correspond with the county societies; to communicate to them beneficial discoveries and improvements; to introduce useful seeds, plants, trees and animals, implements of husbandry, and labor-saving machines; to explore the minerals of the country and to publish periodically the most valuable observations and treatises on husbandry, horticulture, and rural economy. The county societies ought to be enabled to distribute adequate premiums; and a professorship in agriculture connected with the board or attached to the university might also be constituted, embracing the kindred sciences of chemistry and geology, mineralogy, botany, and the other departments of natural history, by which means a complete course of agricultural education would be taught, developing the principles of the science, illustrating the practice of the art, and restoring this first and best pursuit of man to that intellectual rank which it ought to occupy in the scale of human estimation."[38]

In 1819, after regretting the failure of a measure embodying the recommendations of 1818, and asking why the state should encourage the arts and sciences in general, "and agriculture, the most important of all arts, the most useful of all sciences, be alone proscribed from the participation of its bounty," he goes on to say: "The societies already constituted have, by stimulating emulation and diffusing information, affected great good; and if they be assisted in their useful and honorable career, by pecuniary appropriations, and if a board of agriculture, connected with a course of appropriate studies, be instituted, we have every reason to believe that the most beneficial consequences will result in multiplying the products of this country; in increasing the value

---

[38]V. 2, p. 898.

and ameliorating the quality of our commodities; in preventing an undue augmentation of the learned professions, *and in maintaining the equilibrium of society*, by restoring the most numerous calling to its merited intellectual rank."[39]   He then proceeds to recommend that this proposed board of agriculture be given increased powers.

In the speech of January, 1820, there is to be found this comment: "The law which passed at the last session for the encouragement of agriculture has fully realized the patriotic views of the Legislature.   The institution of a board to superintend this important pursuit with authority to receive and communicate useful information, and to dispense the means of valuable improvement will always be considered an important era in our history."   Then not satisfied, he says further: "The excellence of this system, may, however, be greatly improved by extending the duration, augmenting the fund, and enlarging the power of the superintending board."[40]

But bolder still, he recommends (1826) what the twentieth century is only beginning to realize: "I have at various times solicited the attention of the Legislature to the encouragement of agriculture, the first and best pursuit of man; and which in its twofold character, as an art and a science, is susceptible of great improvement, and demands and deserves your fostering patronage. *A wide and unexplored field lies before us.*   Experimental and pattern farms; plantations of useful trees for ship-building, architecture and fuel; labor-saving machines; improved seeds and plants of those productions now used; new modes of cultivation; and the whole range of rural economy are subjects deserving your animating support."[41]

Technical.   Still another means through which this sociological conception finds expression, is given in the message of 1825—this is the most important on this subject: "The Mechanic and Scientific Institute of New York has been established for the purpose of diffusing the benefits of science throughout the various mechanical professions by means of lectures, apparatus, models, books, and public exhibitions of ingenuity, skill, and industry.

[39]V. 2, p. 969.
[40]V. 2, p. 1005.
[41]V. 3, p. 126.

The usefulness of this institution would be greatly enhanced by the erection of an edifice adequate for its purposes; and it is believed that an appropriate site may be concurrently granted by the State and City of New York without inconvenience to either, from contiguous property in that city belonging to both, and now unoccupied. As this is the first organized school of the kind in the world, and is destined to increase the skill, and elevate the character of the mechanical interest, by applying philosophy to the arts, and imparting the benefits of science to that most useful body of our fellow citizens, its claims upon the public bounty will not escape your favorable attention."[42]

Its Support

After noting Clinton's extensive program, it will be interesting to see his attitude toward its support. In 1818, he said: "Funds to the amount of $750,000.00 have been granted to the three colleges, and about $100,000.00 to the incorporated academies. While this liberality reflects honor on the State, it cannot be too forcibly inculcated, nor too generally understood, that in promoting the great interests of moral and intellectual cultivation, there can be no prodigality in the application of public treasure."[43] In January, 1820, he said: "In such a cause, liberality can rarely degenerate into profusion."[44] In 1822, he said: "I am happy to have it in my power to say that this State has always evinced a liberal spirit in the promotion of education, and I am persuaded that no consideration short of total inability will ever prevent similar demonstrations."[45] And so similar recommendations are made in the other messages.

The speech of November, 1820, sums up this point and states its relation to the fundamental thesis: "the whole appropriation for the promotion of education may be estimated at two millions and a half dollars. Although the sum may appear highly liberal, yet when we look at the resources, population and extent of the State, and consider that knowledge is essential to the happiness and dignity of man; to the existence of republican government and to national power and glory, we must feel persuaded that

---

[42]V. 3, p. 67.
[43]V. 2, p. 904. Cf. Elliott's Some Fiscal Aspects of Education, p. 4.
[44]V. 2, p. 1018.
[45]V. 2, p. 1100.

more munificent dispensation ought to be afforded for its encouragement and diffusion."[46]

RESTATEMENT OF PROPOSITION—THE EDUCATIONAL IMPLICATIONS OF DEMOCRACY

The foregoing presentation makes evident the fact that Clinton saw clearly the educational implications of democracy. It may be here indicated again from a somewhat different approach. In the message of 1825, Clinton said: "As connected with these important topics permit me to request your attention to a more accurate definition, a more liberal extension, and more secure enjoyment of the elective franchise. *Without the right of suffrage, liberty cannot exist.* It is the vital principle of representative government, and it ought, therefore, to be effectively fortified against accident, design or corruption."[47] After enumerating the various alternatives necessary to secure the right of suffrage, and pointing to a few illustrations which show the complexity and the liability to fraud and injustice of the present arrangement, he says: "I submit, therefore, to your consideration whether the constitution ought not to be so modified as to render citizenship, full age and competent residence the only requisite qualification."[48]

It is necessary to keep in mind, however, in this connection, the statement of the message of 1827: "But after all the great bulwark of republican government is the cultivation of education and the *right of suffrage cannot be exercised in a salutary manner without intelligence.*"[49] Hence the responsibility of the State, and hence Clinton's elaborate educational program as the chief executive officer of the State.

There is no better concluding paragraph for this chapter than the following from the speech of 1822: "The first duty of a state is to render its citizens virtuous by intellectual instruction and moral discipline, by enlightening their minds, purifying their hearts and teaching them their rights and obligations. Those solid and enduring honors which arise from the cultivation of

---

[46]V. 2, p. 1049.
[47]V. 3, p. 58.
[48]V. 3, p. 59.
[49]V. 3, p. 158.

science and the acquisition and diffusion of knowledge, will out-
live the renown of the statesman and the glory of the warrior;
and if any stimulus were wanting in a case so worthy of all our
attention and patronage, we may find it in the example before
our eyes, of the author of the Declaration of Independence, who
has devoted the evening of his illustrious life to the establishment of an university in his native state."[50]*

---

[50]V. 2, p. 1100.
*Clinton has embodied his views of science mainly in his Phi Beta Kappa
Address and the Introductory Discourse before the Literary and Philosophical
Society, and i cidentally in the Columbia College Alumni and the American
Academy of Arts addresses. He is a thorough Baconian in his attitude to-
ward the significance of science in our social life, in its futility as a mere
science of description and nomenclature, in its possibilities of growth and evo-
lution, and in its method.

CHAPTER IV

SIGNIFICANCE OF CLINTON'S VIEWS

THE COMPREHENSIVENESS OF THE PLAN

The first significant thing to be noted in a statement of Clinton's educational views relates to the extent of his educational scheme—it is its comprehensiveness, both as it relates to grades of instruction included in it, and to the classes of society to profit by it. It includes elementary, secondary, and higher education. It provides means for both males and females, for the poor as well as the rich, for the colored person as well as for the white, for the criminal as well as the law abiding, for the defective as well as the normal, for the deaf and dumb. Of course, it is significant, too, that so much actually secured effective and successful embodiment in institutions, as will be shown.

THE EMPHASIS ON THE LESS FORMAL EDUCATIONAL AGENCIES.

Another significant thing is the emphasis on the less formal educational agencies, on literary, philosophical, and historical societies, on agricultural and horticultural societies, on lyceums of natural histories, and on libraries. Education was thus conceived to be a broader process than school instruction. It thus becomes a social process, in which many and various institutions take part.

AN UNDERLYING EDUCATIONAL SOCIOLOGY

The foregoing points, the comprehensiveness of the scheme, both as it relates to the grades of institutions and to the individuals included under it and the emphasis on the less formal educational agencies, are even more significant when they are unified.

They are, then, found to be after all, only various expressions of a unique pedagogical contribution for the time—an educational sociology.

Education, it is agreed, has both a psychological and a sociological phase; this latter is usually referred to as the ethical, especially by the Herbartians. The objection to the latter term is that it is usually interpreted in terms of the individual rather than of the social. With the psychological phase we have, at this time, nothing to do.

The sociological phase provides pedagogy with its ends. The dominant view all over the world at the beginning of the century was the disciplinary one. Psychical processes were regarded as ends in themselves; the object being the development of certain so-called faculties of imagination, judgment, etc. The subject was as nothing; the discipline, everything. The subject matter was suitable in proportion as it was dull and uninteresting; it was unrelated to the life-needs of the child and the social demands of the time.

As already remarked, the early American statesman had an entirely different conception, which was in the third chapter denominated the sociological. It was there noted that Clinton gave emphatic expression to this view almost continuously during his public career. He regarded it as the duty of the state—and its prime duty—to see to it that the individuals of which it was composed, were enlightened. He definitely set up the proposition, which quite recently has been admirably developed by one of America's leading sociologists, that the state or society acting in its corporate political capacity, should set about to improve itself. In other words, the state's function is the administration of the social estate. The social estate is, in the language of President Butler, the spiritual inheritance of the race. It is society's duty to see that each individual gets his share—that the possibility of inheriting the total social heritage should exist for everyone. Participation in the social inheritance does not diminish it; it increases it, rather.

It was Clinton's purpose to provide for a more general participation in this social inheritance by female as well as by male, by the colored man as well as by the white. It was Clinton's purpose to see that every possible means should be used for the diffusion of this social inheritance, and that new means should be created for its wider diffusion, i.e., lyceums of natural history and historical societies. Looking at these last statements from the other point of view, Clinton recognized clearly that this social inheritance is transmitted not only by the formal educational agencies where there is this conscious effort on society's part, but also in the less formal institutions. Besides clearly recognizing the need and function of these latter institutions in the social economy, he made powerful and persistent efforts to have them increase in number and power. With what success his efforts were attended will appear in succeeding chapters.

PART III

INFLUENCE OF DE WITT CLINTON AND ITS

SIGNIFICANCE

CHAPTER V

THE CONDITIONS AND BASES OF CLINTON'S INFLUENCE

From an educational standpoint, the problem before New York State at the beginning of the nineteenth century, was to provide for an adequate educational environment which would offer to all an opportunity to develop whatever mental powers they possessed, thus producing those men, the leaders and others, who would carry on efficiently the work of society and raise it progressively to higher levels of individual and social achievement.

Modern sociological theory has stated the social problem in the following terms: How shall society, acting in its corporate political capacity, set about consciously to manufacture those agents of civilization, which shall raise the level of social achievement, and how shall society secure the universal distribution of the social heritage? Clinton felt keenly the problem and sought its solution in the establishment of an educational environment, though he probably would not have stated the problem as we do, nor have called his solution an educational environment.

What, then, is an educational environment? In general and in social terms, it is such an environment as will provide the conditions for producing those changes in all individuals which shall best secure social stability and social progress. Or in the terms of the members of society, it is such an environment as is "favorable to the exercise of native powers, and adapted in any given case to the particular quality, shade, or timber those powers may possess."

Concretely, what is such an environment? Lester F. Ward, quoting de Candolle, gives a list of twenty "causes." We shall quote here those applicable to the United States:

73

.

"The existence of numerous families having traditions favorable to science and to intellectual occupations of all kinds."

"Primary, and especially secondary and higher education, well organized and independent of political parties and religious sects, tending to stimulate research and to encourage young persons and professors to devote themselves to science."

"Abundant and well organized facilities for scientific research (libraries, observatories, collections)."

"Public opinion favorable to science and to those who pursue it."

"A large number of scientific societies or academies."[1]

For New York State at the beginning of the nineteenth century the provision of such an environment had to be a creation. The readers of the following sections will see that the purpose of Clinton's educational endeavors is easily and most aptly stated in terms of an educational environment, embodying the foregoing features.

It is particularly difficult at times to determine how far Clinton is responsible for the educational achievements and movements of his time in New York State. The following evidence shows that Clinton had the power, or at least, that his contemporaries believed that he had the power (the second chapter contains the evidence that he had the inclination), to determine and, in a large measure, control, the trend of events.

During his ten years in the State Legislature, practically every piece of educational legislation was referred to him. Almost every legislative bill bearing on education which became a law was introduced by him. Other evidence is found in Clinton's correspondence. The chairman of the Board of Trustees of Columbia College, appeals to Clinton in the interest of a measure as follows: "Your assistance in accelerating its accomplishment is highly desirable and can hardly fail to be decisive."[2] The good old Quaker, John Murray, Jr., writes to Clinton as follows: "And although we are unwilling to trespass too much on thy time, yet as we have reason to believe, it was through thy exertions the bill for incorporating the Manumission Society passed the

---

[1]Ward's Applied Sociology, p. 146. Almost all the factors not mentioned are not applicable to American conditions or are already secured, e. g., a clergy not restricted to celibacy; or they are such as cannot be produced if absent, e. g., a geographical position under a temperate or northern climate.

[2]L. to C., v. 4, p. 55.

Senate last session, we cannot forbear to solicit thy renewed attentions to that subject. Thy interest with some of the leading members of the Assembly may be conducive to the passing of the bill."[3] Nor was the social influence of Clinton hardly less decisive, at least in the opinion of his contemporaries, than his political influence. A. Hyde Neuville, when organizing the Economical School Society, wrote to Clinton, "Deign, Sir, to place your name first on the list of actual members of the society—it will assure the success of the institution."[4]

Though this evidence is probably sufficient to establish the point, it may be well, by way of confirmation, to quote Mr. McBain's conclusions in his study of certain political aspects of Clinton's career. These conclusions are stated in several places; two are selected for quotation. Mr. McBain says:

"His coming into his own as leader of the Republican party (1801) in his State had not been accomplished without commotion, but his conduct in the controversy which developed served to exhibit at once his weakness and his strength as a politician. He never showed any great power in the handling of men, and his inability to hit upon a working basis with Jay was an illustration of his tactlessness, but in every great movement of his life he manifested an overmastering belief in himself which carried conviction to those around him, and the loyalty with which his party supported him in 1801 was an evidence of his ability to command a following that was not wholly personal."[5]

"It was in this position as one of the members of the Council of Appointment that De Witt Clinton came to be recognized as perhaps the dominant factor in New York politics. Many had held the position before without achieving fame or power. But the moment was critical, the council was small, a majority of the members were of the triumphant incoming party and the political power which lay potentially in the hands of that council was enormous. It was easy to see that under such circumstances a man of Clinton's overtopping personality came into the exercise of his own strength."[6]

The influence of Clinton is largely the influence of a group. Clinton was prominently connected with two groups of individuals, the one mainly philanthropic, the other mainly scientific. Repre-

[3]L. to C., v. 3, p. 64.
[4]L. to C., v. 4, p. 48.
[5]McBain's De Witt Clinton and the Origin of the Spoils System, p. 96.
[6]*Ibid.,* p. 77.

sentatives of the former group were the Quakers: Thomas Eddy
and the Murrays; representatives of the latter were Doctors
Hosack and Mitchell.   The typical institution of the first was the
Free School Society; the typical institution of the second was the
Literary and Philosophical Society.   The point here—apart from
Clinton's identity with both groups—is that while it would be
manifestly unfair to give the fellow-workers and co-laborers, the
"talent" of praise, it would be also manifestly unfair not to give
them any.   To Clinton the main award is given because in these
respective groups, he was the dominant and the dominating personality.   The remainder of this chapter is evidence of the truth
of this contention.

Another way of expressing the thoughts of the preceding
paragraphs is that the influence of Clinton was largely the influence of the societies which he organized, for which he secured
incorporation and legislative grants, and which he assisted both
pecuniarily and with his more valuable services.   Ultimately, however, this is simply saying that he had tremendous political power
and that he used it beneficently.   Then apart from this political
power he was an active and zealous worker as a member of these
societies, so much so that his colleagues in recognition of his unusual ability and his equally unusual breadth of information, raised
him to the highest office in their gift.   He was President of the
Free School Society, the Literary and Philosophical Society, the
New York Historical Society, the Antiquarian Society, the American Academy of Arts and Sciences, the American Bible Society,
and the Presbyterian Education Society.

A rather striking testimonial to the stimulus which Clinton
gave to the intellectual life of the community in his election as
honorary member of numerous learned societies.   With most of
these, strange to say, his connection was not merely formal.   He
was in frequent correspondence with the officers of these societies,
making many valuable suggestions.   Only a general statement of his connection with these societies can be given.

He was an honorary member of four of the county agricultural
societies, and of three agricultural societies of other states.   He
was, too, an honorary member of four lyceums of natural history
in New York State, and of the Western Museum Society.   He
was a corresponding member of the Academy of Natural Science

of Philadelphia, and a member of the American Geological Society, and the American Academy of Arts and Sciences (Boston).

His interest was not confined to the scientific societies, but extended to the philosophical, literary and historical societies. He was a member of several literary and philosophical societies, including the American Philosophical Society of Philadelphia, and the Literary and Philosophical Society of New York. He was a corresponding member of the Massachusetts Historical Society. His connection with the New York Historical Society will be indicated in some detail later. He was identified in several capacities with the American Antiquarian Society and the American Bible Society.

CHAPTER VI

CLINTON'S INFLUENCE ON THE LESS FORMAL EDUCATIONAL AGENCIES

NEW YORK HISTORICAL SOCIETY

It is not possible to trace Clinton's connections with the various societies of which he was a member. In some cases the material is not existent, or if existent, is not generally accessible or known; in other cases it would be unprofitable. His relations with the New York Historical Society are treated in detail because his influence here is typical, and because of the general educational influence exerted by the society through its collections, its meetings and its publications.

The minutes of the first meeting show Clinton to have been one of the eleven founders. The minutes are given below:[1]

"NEW YORK, November 20, 1804.
"The following persons, vizt:—Egbert Benson, De Witt Clinton, Rev. William Linn, Rev. Samuel Miller, Rev. John N. Abeel, Rev. John M. Mason, Doctor David Hosack, Anthony Bleeker, Samuel Bayard, Peter G. Stuyvesant and John Pintard, being assembled in the Picture Room of the City Hall of the City of New York, agreed to form themselves into a society, the principal design of which should be to collect and preserve whatever may relate to the natural, civil or ecclesiastical History of the United States in general, and of this state in particular, and appointed Mr. Benson, Doctor Miller, and Mr. Pintard, a committee to prepare and report a draft of the constitution."

The next meeting of the society was held Monday evening, December 10, of the same year. De Witt Clinton was present

---

[1]Reproduced in Kelby's The New York Historical Society, 1804-1904, pp. 1-2.

at this meeting. A constitution was adopted, the institution was given its present name, and officers were elected.

It may be well at this point to state the offices held by Clinton in the society. He was a member of the "Standing Committee," 1808-09; second vice president, 1810-15; first vice president, 1816; and president, 1817-1819.[2] Clinton delivered the discourse at the anniversary meeting of the society, December 6, 1815. The subject of the discourse was "The Iroquois."[3]

Clinton's other services may now be briefly indicated. On February 1, 1809, the petition of Egbert Benson, praying for incorporation, was received in the Senate and referred to a select committee, consisting of Messrs. Clinton, Comstock and Taylor. On February 2, 1809, Mr. Clinton reported and brought in a bill embodying the prayer of the petitioners. It was read a first time and by unanimous consent a second time, and referred to a committee of the whole and ordered engrossed. The entry for the next day, February 3, is after the third reading "the bill do pass." It was amended in the Assembly, February 9, and passed as amended with the concurrence of the Senate, February 10, 1809.

On March 20, 1810, a petition from the Society praying the Legislature to grant them such aid as shall be meet and the general interest of the State permit, was received. Clinton looked after the interests of the bill in the Senate, where it passed. He sent the following letter to Mr. Pintard, secretary of the society, on the day it passed:

"ALBANY, March 22, 1810.

"DEAR SIR:

"I have the pleasure of informing you that the bill for endowing the Historical Society and killing the wolves and panthers, passed the Senate this morning without opposition. If the Federal Assembly shall act as liberally as the Republican Senate, it will go through, but I am fearful that your party will be very deficient in this respect.

"The Mechanics' Bank bill has passed the Senate with equal unanimity.

"I am, dear sir, yours sincerely,

"DE WITT CLINTON."

"John Pintard, Esq."

---

[2] Cf. Kelby.
[3] Given in Campbell's Life and Writings of De Witt Clinton.

Mr. S. L. Mitchell proves Clinton's fear well grounded, for he writes under date of April 3, 1810: "The vote in spite of all that the friends of the project could say was '43 to 27.' "

The following resolution was passed at a meeting held January 11, 1814:

"Resolved, That application be made to the Legislature of this State for their patronage of this society, and that Mr. Clinton be appointed to draft a suitable memorial on the subject."

"At the next quarterly meeting held April 12th, Mr. Clinton informed the Society that, agreeably to their request at the last meeting he had drawn up a memorial to the Legislature of this State for their patronage which he presented at the present sessions of both Houses. That a clause granting this society $12,000, which was included in the bill entitled 'An act for instituting a lottery for the promotion of Literature,' had passed the Senate, but was non-concurred in the House of Assembly. Ayes 41, nays 44.

"The act became a law on April 15, 1814."

The society a little later, 1816, established a mineralogical cabinet. The most zealous workers in this direction of the society's work were Dr. Mitchell, De Witt Clinton and Colonel George Gibbs. In 1829, this aspect of the society's work had become so large and tended to overshadow the main work of the society, that it was dropped and the collection was presented to the Lyceum of Natural History.

In his message to the Legislature in 1826, Clinton made the following recommendation with reference to the Historical Society:

"The charter of the Historical Society of New York has expired, and its finances are in a state of great depression. Its collections of books, manuscripts, medals and maps, illustrative of the antiquities and history of our country, are very valuable and ought to be preserved for the public benefit. The resuscitation of this society, and a liberal provision for its extended usefulness are measures worthy of your adoption."

The recommendation resulted in the passing of "An act for renewing and continuing in force an act entitled An act to incorporate the New York Historical Society, passed February 10, 1809." This act passed February 10, 1826,[4] and remained in force until February 10, 1839. The message of 1827, says:

---

[4]Chap. 41, Laws of 1826.

"The charter of the New York Historical Society which had expired by its own limitation was renewed at the last session, but without the pecuniary aid that was solicited and which would have been worthily bestowed, considering the light which its researches and collections have shed on the history of America in general, and of this state in particular.

"In 1814 the Historical Society addressed a memorial to the Legislature, wherein it indicated several places for important acquisitions . . . . and it would be very useful to obtain transcripts of all public documents in those quarters which may elucidate our annals in their aboriginal and colonial state."

An act embodying these recommendations was passed March 1, 1827.[5]

LYCEUMS OF NATURAL HISTORY

Another kind of institution and a new factor in the educational environment with which Clinton chose to identify himself was the lyceum of natural history. In a letter (1823) to James Smith, an English scientist of the time, referring to certain letters of his own, written in a "session of great pressure of official business," he says: "My object was to attract public attention to Natural Science and our internal resources."[6] In another letter (1815) he says: "Having been engaged since my youth in the active scenes of political life, I have had little time for scientific investigation, but I have never ceased to hold in the highest respect those men who devote themselves to the acquisition and propagation of knowledge, and the most pleasing retrospect of my past life arises from my having had it sometimes in my power to promote with effectiveness the interests of Science."[7]

Judging from Clinton's scientific views and his personal interest in scientific work, it is natural to expect that he would encourage and lend his powerful assistance to institutions for the encouragement of scientific investigation and the spread of scientific knowledge. And this expectation is borne out by the facts, though previously the Legislature had not given aid to such institutions; at least in the "Index to Laws, 1777-1857, State of New York," I find no law affecting a lyceum of natural history or a similar institution before Clinton's first year as Governor.

---

[5]Chap. 51, Laws of 1827.
[6]L. B., v. 5, June 4, 1823.
[7]L. B., v. 2, p. 259.

Before referring to the laws, it may be well to introduce one of Clinton's letters dated from Albany, December 4, 1823, and addressed to Charles Dewey, Esquire, of Pittsfield, Massachusetts. After thanking him for the Rev. Mr. Hitchcock's discourse on the "Utility of Natural Science," Clinton goes on to say:

"I see you have established a Lyceum of Natural History in Pittsfield. Institutions of this kind are appreciated and have met with considerable encouragement. They are admirably calculated to elicit a spirit of accurate observation and rational inquiry, and the collections which they form will establish the ground-work of important results."[8]

On April 20, 1818, there was passed "An act to incorporate the Lyceum of Natural History in the City of New York."[9]   Other acts were passed to incorporate the Troy Lyceum of Natural History, March 7, 1820,[10] the Hudson Lyceum of Natural History, March 9, 1821,[11] the Catskill Lyceum of Natural History, February 28, 1822,[12] the Delaware Chemical and Geological Society, April 12, 1822,[13] the Utica Lyceum, January 21, 1826,[14] and the New York Atheneum on April 17, of the same year.[15]   During the interim between Clinton's first period of service and his second (in 1823), the Albany Lyceum of Natural History was incorporated.

The impetus given to the movement at its beginning carried it on for many years. In 1830 we find, for example, a law incorporating the Rochester Atheneum, and in 1832, a similar law for the Buffalo Lyceum. During this decade we find laws giving legal status to the following institutions: Brooklyn Lyceum (two laws, 1834, 1835), Schenectady Lyceum and Academy, York Literary and Scientific Institute, and the New York Museum of Natural History. Several similar laws were passed during the next decade (1841-1850), and in 1857 we find two acts connected with what is probably the most famous of these scientific institutes: Cooper Union.

---

[8]L. B., v. 5, Dec. 4, 1823.
[9]Chap. 197, Laws of 1818.
[10]Chap. 62, Laws of 1820.
[11]Chap. 83, Laws of 1821.
[12]Chap. 41, Laws of 1822.
[13]Chap. 181, Laws of 1822.
[14]Chap. 18, Laws of 1826.
[15]Chap. 285, Laws of 1826.

One of the lyceums of natural history is worthy of detailed notice—the first to be incorporated—the Lyceum of Natural History in the City of New York. This is interesting apart from the facts that Clinton was an honorary member of it, and that it was before this society that Samuel L. Mitchill discoursed on the "Character and Scientific Attainments of De Witt Clinton," on July 14, 1828. This lyceum continues to-day as the Academy of Sciences. It holds general meetings and monthly meetings by sections. It publishes annals in octavo and memoirs in quarto, and has a library numbering 18,000 titles. There is an alliance of the academy and numerous scientific societies.[16]

LIBRARIES

Clinton clearly perceived that libraries were important elements in the educational environment. His conception was possibly too far in advance of the time and the conditions to secure adequate practical embodiment. Clinton was impressed as to the value of mercantile libraries and encouraged them whenever the opportunity offered itself. He was probably more forcibly impressed by the value to the community of a public library, the so-called district library in its midst, but his energetic efforts in behalf of such libraries were fruitless, until 1835, seven years after his death.

But Clinton's great service to the library movement is found in his service in connection with the origin and early growth of the State Library. This library was instituted during Clinton's second year as Governor. He selected the original list of books, was chairman of the Board of Trustees during the first decade of its history, and during this period recommended and secured legislation providing adequate financial support for the library and widening its scope, and as Governor signed all such legislation. But Clinton probably never dreamed of the possibilities of the institution as realized to-day.

The State Library. The State Library was instituted[17] during Governor Clinton's first administration. The law, "An act for

[16]Cf., Cattell's Scientific Societies and Associations, p. 8, *in* Butler's Education in the United States, p. 872.

[17]"The necessity for a State Library was undoubtedly forced upon the State by a policy originated by Massachusetts some years before the formation of the library of an interstate exchange of State documents, and the action of

the establishment of a public library at the seat of government," was passed April 21, 1818.[18]   Section one of this law provides that the governor, lieutenant governor, chancellor, and a chief justice of the Supreme Court, shall constitute a board of trustees, and it shall be their duty to cause to be fitted up some proper room in the capitol for the use of the government and the people of this State, and it shall be the duty of the said trustees "to cause to be expended the money appropriated by this act, or which may be hereafter appropriated in fitting up such room and in the purchase of such books, maps and other literary publications for the use of said library as they may deem expedient."   Section two provides for the appointment of a librarian by the trustees, "who shall receive whatever compensation they shall determine," and it provides further that "no book shall at any time be taken from the library for any purpose whatever."   Section three provides for an appropriation of three thousand dollars and an annual appropriation of five hundred dollars to carry into effect the provision of the act.

"An act to enable the Trustees of the State Library to carry into effect a resolution of the Senate and Assembly, authorizing them to purchase one of Theo. Newell's astronomical machines," was passed January 14, 1820.   The act provided for an appropriation of one thousand dollars.[19]

The next law was passed April 18, 1825, and was "An act for the gradual enlargement of the New York State Library, and more effectually to promote the purposes for which it was established."[20]   Section one of this act provides for an appropriation of one thousand dollars for the purchase of books and maps for the use of the library and for fitting up and repairing the room or rooms in which the books are kept.   Section two provides that the "assistant register of the Court of Chancery shall pay from a fund in his charge, to the trustees of the State Library, three hundred dollars annually, for the gradual increase of said library, provided, however, that if the interests or profits do meet the con-

Congress in distributing certain Congressional documents to all States."
Frank Tolman, Reference Librarian, N. Y. State Library.—[A personal letter.]

[18]Chap. 276, Laws of 1818.
[19]Chap. 4, Laws of 1820.
[20]Chap. 203, Laws of 1825.

tingent expenses of the court, the appropriation shall be reduced."
Section three provides that the contingent expenses of the library
shall be paid by the treasurer when duly certified to by a majority
of the trustees. The fourth section of the act provides for an annual report to the Legislature informing it how the money is expended, together with "a true and perfect catalogue of all the
books, maps and charts then remaining within and belonging to
said library." The remaining sections of the act provide for the
repeal of the second section of the Act of April 21, 1818, and in
its place there is substituted a provision permitting members of
Legislature during sessions of the Legislature, of Senate only, or
of the Court of Errors, under proper rules, etc., to take to their
boarding houses or private rooms any books belonging to said
library except such books as trustees believe shall be always kept
at the library for reference. It provides, further, that no more
than two volumes may be taken at once, and that the President of
the Senate and the Speaker of the Assembly shall not give a member his certificate of attendance unless he has returned all books
he has borrowed from the library and settled all accounts in the
way of fines and otherwise.

The last act passed during Clinton's administration was an act
providing for an appropriation of one thousand dollars, to be expended by the trustees for books, maps, and charts. Section two
provides for an annual appropriation of one thousand dollars for
the gradual enlargement of such library.[21]

The history of the State Library may be viewed also from the
standpoint of the Reports of the Trustees. The first report
follows:[22]

THE TRUSTEES OF THE PUBLIC LIBRARY established in the
Capitol respectfully report:
That in pursuance of the act passed at the last session entitled
"An act for the establishment of a public library at the seat of
government," the Board of Trustees constituted by that act have
caused to be fitted up a room in the Capitol for the reception of a
library and have selected and purchased upwards of six hundred
volumes of books proper for such an establishment.[23] They have

---

[21]Chap. 293, Laws of 1827.
[22]A. J., 1819, p. 148.
[23]Mr. Tolman, Reference Librarian of the State Library, says in a private
letter: "The first books purchased by the library were selected largely by
him." [De Witt Clinton.]

endeavored to make such selections within the means provided as in their judgment would best meet the views of the Legislature and correspond with the character of the State.

The catalogue of the books and maps together with the sums expended for the same and for the requisite preparations and accommodations in the Library Room will appear in the annexed schedules.

All of which is respectfully submitted.

DE WITT CLINTON,
JOHN TAYLOR,
JAMES KENT.

The final paragraph of the report for 1825—also signed by De Witt Clinton, is:

"It gives the trustees great pleasure to state that this infant institution, under the fostering care of the Legislature, promises to realize the expectations of the founders and to extend its usefulness throughout the State."

The last report signed by Clinton, was the report for the year ending December 31, 1827. In this report we find this summary of the possessions of the library:

191 volumes Folios.
154 volumes Quartos.
2,301 volumes Octavos.
99 volumes Duodecimos.
15 volumes Decimo Sexto.
2,760 Books.
23 Maps.
4 Charts.
12 Portrait Prints.
1 Bust.[24]

The report of 1828—signed by Mr. Van Buren, as chairman—includes in the possessions of the library "1 Monumental Engraving (De Witt Clinton)."[25]

Other Libraries. Herbert Adams, in his "Public Libraries and Popular Education," says:[26] "The school district library of the State of New York is a good historic starting point for American popular education in connection with libraries." On the following page we find this statement: "In the report of the Department

---

[24] S. J., 1828.
[25] A. J., 1829.
[26] p. 96.

of Public Instruction for 1889, it is said that New York State was the first to undertake to establish libraries as factors in educational work. De Witt Clinton was the father of the idea."

Clinton, after commenting on the fact that he is deeply impressed with the momentous relation of this department of our social policy (i.e., education) to the cardinal interests of the State, in his message to the Legislature in 1825, goes on to say: "In furtherance of this invaluable system, I recommend . . . the introduction *and the distribution of useful books."* This last idea is made more definite in his 1827 message, where he recommends "small and suitable collections of books and maps attached to our common schools are worthy of attention when it is remembered that objects of this description, enter into the very formation of our characters, control our destinies through life, and protect the freedom and advance the glory of countries."

These recommendations had no immediate effect, but reinforced by the efforts of Dix, Flagg and others, they were embodied in the law of 1835—the first law authorizing a community to tax itself to establish and maintain public libraries. It may be stated in the words of Mr. Dix, "the object was not so much for children attending schools, as for those who have completed their common school education. Its main design was to throw into school districts and places within reach of all their inhabitants, a collection of good works on subjects calculated to enlarge their understanding and store their minds with useful knowledge."[27]

However, school libraries intended for the pupils had long before been established by the Free School Society. In the fourteenth annual report, April 30, 1819, is this statement; "Libraries have been recently annexed to each of our schools, consisting of books of Voyages, Travels, Histories, etc., which are to be circulated among those scholars who, for their progress in learning, are deserving of reward." The remainder of the paragraph is taken up in soliciting donations of books.

One other important phase of library work is the organization

---

[27]Cf. p. 100. "Though the free public library is now the prevailing type in the United States, the school district type is worthy of commemoration because it marks pioneer influence in many individual American commonwealths and the recognized principles that the library is a feature of public education and deserves to be supported like common schools by public taxation. It is not enough for a community to educate its children; it should educate itself. The public library *is for all, adults, as well as children."*

of mechanics' libraries. Clinton's attitude toward these institutions is indicated in the following letter, dated from Albany, Dec. 11, 1826, and addressed to W. Wood, Esq., Canandaigua:

"SIR:

"I hear with no common gratification that it is in contemplation to establish a library in the flourishing village of Canandaigua for the benefit of young men engaged in mercantile and other business or who are desirous of devoting a portion of their time to the acquisition of useful information. Fully impressed with the benefit of such institutions; also believing that they have derived their impulse in a great measure from your benevolent exertions, in behalf of Mrs. Clinton and myself I ask from you the favor to present to that library the books accompanying this communication as a testimonial of our high respects for the principles and of our own best wishes for its success.

"Blair's Lectures, 3 vols. for myself,

"Blair's Sermons, 2 vols. for Mrs. C."[28]

---

[28]L. B., v. 8, p. 53.

CHAPTER VII

INFLUENCE ON FORMAL EDUCATION

COMMON SCHOOL EDUCATION

The Public School Society

Great as was Clinton's influence in connection with the establishment and progress of learned societies, lyceums of natural history, and libraries, it is almost entirely overshadowed by the far-reaching consequences of his connection with the Public School Society and the various minor school societies.

One relying mainly on Bourne's "History of the Public School Society," would come away from a careful perusal of that work with something like the following as a statement of De Witt Clinton's relation to the society:

Clinton was not present at the first meeting of the twelve founders of the Free School Society at John Murray's house on Pearl Street, on February 19, 1805. However, Clinton and thirty-five others were, by the act of April 9, 1805,[1] constituted a body corporate under the title of "A Society for establishing a Free School in the City of New York, for the education of such poor children as do not belong to or are not provided for by any religious society." The second section of the act constituted Clinton and the original twelve a Board of Trustees, until the regular election. At the regular election May 6, 1805, Clinton was elected president, to which office he was annually re-elected until his death in 1828. An address to the public, dated May 18, 1805, soliciting aid, was issued in the name of the trustees.[2]

---

[1]Chap. 108, Laws of 1805.
[2]Bourne's History of the Public School Society, pp. 6-8.

De Witt Clinton headed this list with the largest donation—$200.[3] He made a long address, which Mr. Bourne prints entire, at the dedication of the new school building, December 11, 1809.[4] The next reference we find to Clinton is his offering of a resolution (December, 1818), granting permission to Joseph Lancaster to use the schoolrooms of the society at such times as they were not being used for instruction, for the purpose of delivering lectures.[5] His name is subscribed along with the other trustees to an address to the parents and guardians of children belonging to schools under the care of the New York Free School Society, dated April 9, 1819. The reader may wonder, for no explanation is given, that later documents quoted in the work are signed by the Vice President for the Trustees and not by the President. The last reference but one to Clinton comes in connection with the Bethel School controversy, i.e., relating to the distribution of the Common School Fund in support of sectarian education. The original bill was amended in the Assembly to vest in the corporation of the City of New York the power of distributing school moneys in such manner as they, in their wisdom, shall think proper. The Free School Society's committee not having instructions from their constituents, did not know what to do; they consulted Clinton, who advised them that they would not be warranted in an opposition which would embarrass the passage of the bill, and they accordingly gave their assent to the proposed amendment.[6] The bill became a law November 19, 1824. The last reference is the resolution on the death of Clinton, which may be given here most conveniently:

"The Trustees of the Public School Society being informed of the sudden decease of His Excellency De Witt Clinton, who among his other testimonials of public esteem and confidence has held the office of President of this Society from its first organization.

"Resolved, As the sense of this board that while it is our duty to bend with unmurmuring submission to the will of Divine Providence, we view this event as a signal calamity to our country, to the cause of science and public improvement, and the many useful institutions of which the deceased was a distinguished ornament and a patron. That he occupied a large place in the

---

[3]Bourne, p. 8.
[4]*Ibid.*, pp. 14-24.
[5]*Ibid.*, p. 32.
[6]*Ibid.*, p. 74.

affection and respect of his countrymen, as one of the most able and successful benefactors; and that, as connected with this and similar associations, the cause of literature and benevolence has sustained in his death and unspeakable and irreparable loss."[7]

An examination of the sources shows that the foregoing account is very unsatisfactory and incomplete.

After incorporation, an address was issued May 18, 1805, asking for funds. Clinton contributed, as already noted, the largest sum, $200, and his name appears first on the list of subscribers. The original list is preserved in the files of the New York Historical Society.[8] There is also in the possession of the New York Historical Society, a copy of the list of original "subscribers to the New York Free School Society obtained by De Witt Clinton, Esq., and Frederick De Peyster, in the First Ward." The total amount collected in this ward was $5,820.

On March 21, 1806,[9] the memorial of De Witt Clinton, president of the "Society for establishing a Free School in the City of New York, for the education of such poor children as do not belong to or are not provided for by any religious society," praying that the time for holding meetings may be discretionary with the trustees, rather than prescribed as now, was read. Mr. Clinton asked leave to bring in a bill embodying the object prayed for in the memorial. Leave being granted, Clinton brought in an appropriate bill, in the form of an act to amend the original bill. The bill was read a first time, and by unanimous consent, was read a second time, and was referred to a committee of the whole. On March 24, 1806, Mr. Graham reported the bill from the committee of the whole without amendment. It was read a third time and passed March 25, 1806. It passed the Assembly April 2, 1806, and to the Council of Revision it did "not appear improper that it should become a law."[10]

On February 3, 1809, a memorial from the trustees of what, during the following year, was known as the Free School Society praying legislative aid, was read and referred to Messrs. Clinton (chairman), Taylor and Graham. Two weeks later (February

---

[7]Bourne, p. 109.
[8]This list is reproduced in Palmer's History of the New York Public Schools.
[9]This and the following references can be readily found in the *Senate Journal,* under the dates given.
[10]Chap. 125, Laws of 1806.

17) Clinton reported as follows: "That the committee are of opinion that until aid can be afforded from the fund allotted to common schools, it is highly expedient and proper for the Legislature to assist the said institution in some other shape: That under this impression (they) pray for leave to introduce a bill." Leave being granted, Clinton introduced a bill called "An act for the encouragement of the Free School in the City of New York," which provided for the payment out of the excise money of four thousand dollars to the Trustees for a new building and of one thousand dollars annually until the pleasure of the Legislature shall otherwise determine. It was read twice and referred to a committee of the whole. On February 20, the bill was read a third time and passed. The memorial was read in the Assembly on February 3, 1807, and referred to a select committee of which Mr. Rutgers was chairman and after the usual procedure became a law, February 27, 1807.[11]

To any one following the history of the society, which was at successive periods known as (1) the Society for Establishing a Free School in the City of New York, for the education of such children as do not belong to or are not provided for by any religious society, 1805-1808; (2) the Free School Society (1808-1825); and (3) the Public School Society (1825-1853), it must be evident that the society could not have developed and become the tremendous factor it did in New York education, if indeed it could have lived, had it not been so liberally and frequently assisted by the Legislature and the Common Council of the city, but especially the former. It must appear, too, to any one following the facts as they are presented here, for example, that without Clinton's powerful assistance, it is very doubtful if such aid would have been forthcoming. At any rate this is the opinion of the Trustees, and two letters written by John Murray, Jr., could be introduced to support the statement, and as directly bearing on our main topic. One is given in full:

"NEW YORK, 1st mo. 29, 1807.
"RESPECTED FRIEND, DE WITT CLINTON:
"I am requested by the Trustees of the New York Free School to forward to thy care, a Memorial which they have prepared ad-

―――――――――
[11]Chap. 20, Laws of 1807.

dressed to the Legislature and which thou wilt please to present accordingly, a copy will be forwarded to Col. Rutgers in order for him to lay the same before the Assembly. As the subject is one which thou hast manifested a zeal to promote we need not say more than to repeat our confidence in thy further exertions for the promotion of an Institution which is admitted to be of great importance to the Community at large, and perhaps the Mayor cannot exert his influence in any department, civil or religious in a cause more laudable or useful.

"And although we are unwilling to trespass too much on thy time, yet as we have reason to believe it was through thy exertions the bill for incorporating the Manumission Society passed the Senate last session we can not forbear to solicit thy renewed attention to that subject. Thy interest with some leading members of the Assembly may be greatly conducive to the passing of the bill which we understood would probably have got through the House had it not been neglected and put off to a late period in the session; therefore should early attention be given to the subject, and the bill called up by some influential members, perhaps it might be got through without much opposition. . . . .

"thy aft friend,

"JOHN MURRAY JUN."[12]

The other letter dated March 12, 1808, simply reinforces this last one.[13]

Valuable supplementary material has been found in the minutes of the Common Council of New York City. During 1807 a resolution was passed granting the request of the Trustees of the New York Free School Society for the use of twenty feet of the Bridewell yard joining their school house for privies. On January 18, 1808, the Committee of the Corporation appointed to confer with the Committee of the Free School, reported as follows: After assigning other property for the State arsenal, the report goes on:

"That the State shall assent to this arrangement it will be expedient to grant the new building and suitable adjacent ground to the Trustees of the Free School to be occupied as long as they use same for the purpose of their Institution and on the express condition that the said Trustees shall educate the children of the Alms House gratuitously.

"The committee confidently recommend this plan. It will accommodate the State in a more public and spacious arsenal. It will accommodate the corporation in the education of their poor

---

[12]L. to C., v. 3, p. 64.
[13]L. to C., v. 4, p. 19.

children. It will accommodate the Trustees of the Free School with a convenient place and it will redound to the corporation and the general good of the community in the means it will afford for the diffusion of knowledge among the necessitous, an object of the first importance and which has hitherto been neglected in this city particularly as it respects the poor children under the care of the corporation.

> "J. D. MILLER,
> "JACOB MOTT,
> "JASPER WARD."

"Jan. 18, 1808."[14]

It is always difficult to point out just what influence a presiding officer exerts, and Clinton's case as presiding officer of the Council is no exception. One may be sure that he manifested the same zeal here as he did at Albany. The only concrete piece of evidence available is his letter from Albany, dated March 25, 1808.

"SIR:

"I send you by Mr. Fairlie for the information of the Common Council three papers printed by the State printers which contain most of the acts passed this session that apply immediately to the City of New York. These acts being published officially are sufficiently authenticated for every purpose that may be wanted by the Common Council.

"The Common Council will observe that no notice will be taken in the Act for the erection of a new arsenal of the intended appropriation of the present one for the use of the Free School. This was considered as an arrangement proper to be made by the Common Council and the Trustees of that establishment without the interference of the Legislature, but it has been fully understood that the design of the corporation as expressed in that memorial will be fully carried into effect. The Free School is undoubtedly one of the most useful institutions we have, and I have no doubt will receive additional patronage from the corporation. To prevent any further misunderstanding I would recommend that the agreement between the Council and the Trustees of the Free School be reduced to writing and signed. . . . .

"I am, etc.,

> "DE WITT CLINTON."

"P. C. VAN DYCK, ESQ."[14]

During March, 1808, the Trustees of the Free School Society in the City of New York prayed for certain changes in their act

---

[14]Minutes of the Common Council (Ms.).

of incorporation and for legislative aid, which prayer was read and referred to a select committee, consisting of Messrs. Denning, Adams and Coe. On March 18, Mr. Denning reported favorably, using the words of the memorial which had been written by Clinton.

The bill embodying the change was introduced and read a first time and by unanimous consent was read a second time and referred to a committee of the whole. The next day Mr. Taylor, from the committee on the whole, reported the bill and it was ordered engrossed. On March 21, it was read a third time and passed. The bill was passed in the Assembly, March 29, and became a law April 1, 1808.[15] Although it appears Clinton had absolutely nothing to do with this act so far as the legislative record goes, still we know from Mr. Murray's letter that his influence was potent.

On February 3, 1810, the Trustees of the Free School Society presented a memorial for legislative aid and for certain alterations in their act of incorporation. It was read and referred to a select committee, consisting of Messrs. Clinton (chairman), McLean and Hall. Clinton, on March 23, 1810, reported that the prayers of the petitioners ought to be granted, and asked leave to bring in a bill, which bill was introduced, read twice and referred to a committee of the whole on March 2, 1810, and ordered engrossed. It passed the Senate the next day. It became a law March 24, 1810.[16] The law provided that members of the society who paid fifty dollars would be entitled to send one child to the school. It appropriated four thousand dollars. It permitted the appointment of not more than five additional trustees.

The memorial of the Trustees of the Free School Society, stating that it is in the power of the Legislature without any interference with the revenue of the State, to contribute essentially to the great object of the society and praying for the patronage of the Legislature, was read (March 2, 1811), and on motion of Clinton it was ordered that leave be given to present a bill. In accordance with such leave Clinton brought in a bill entitled "An act for the further encouragement of free schools in the City of New York." The bill was read twice at this meeting, ordered

---

[15]Chap. 111, Laws of 1808.
[16]Chap. 214, Laws of 1810.

engrossed on the sixth, and was read the third time, and passed on the seventh. It passed the Assembly on the twenty-ninth and became a law April 1, 1811.[17] This act provided that out of the excise funds there shall be paid to the Trustees of the Free School Society, "the sum of four thousand dollars for the purpose of erecting another building; and for every year thereafter, until the pleasure of the Legislature shall otherwise determine, there shall be paid to the said trustees out of the said fund in addition to the annual sums heretofore granted, the sum of five hundred dollars for the purpose of promoting the benevolent objects of the said corporation."

The next step taken by the Legislature was a decisive one; it related to the distribution of the Common School Fund. Before the details are given a general statement may be permitted in this connection. It is difficult to point out in detail just what influence Clinton had, though there can be no doubt that as in all educational questions he exercised very great influence—much more than we can now trace. Says Renwick in his "Life of De Witt Clinton":[18] "In almost all his messages to the Legislature this important subject (common school education) held a prominent place, and there are abundant reasons for believing that it is in a measure owing to his constant exertion and his unwearied perseverance that the school fund, and the common schools are at the present time in so flourishing a condition."

A letter from the father of the Common School Fund, Jedidiah Peck, reinforces the preceding statement. The letter follows:

"BURLINGTON, March 9, 1810.
"DEAR SIR:
"Your obliging favor of the second ultimo did not come to hand until last evening with its inclosure. I thank you for the present and compliment you have paid me on the score of the common school funds: it gratifies me to find the funds are increasing. I anticipate great advantage in the diffusion of useful knowledge from them amongst the lower order of the people. I have read your address with peculiar satisfaction; and am glad to hear you are making such strides in improvement and extension in the education of poor children in the common school; although I stood in need of no further obligations from you to give me perfect

---

[17]An Account of the Free School Society of New York, p. 33. All the laws to 1814 are quoted in full.

[18]p. 35.

satisfaction, that you would do all in your power that was reasonable to protect and preserve those funds for the uses they were appropriated for. When I left the Legislature you voluntarily gave me your word of honor that you would be a guardian of the common school funds; this was satisfactory to me and when I have heard some one speak doubtfully as to the common people reaping any benefit from them I have observed that you had engaged to support and guard those funds and that I did not doubt but we should yet reap the benefit of them. It is true as you say while in the Legislature I watched with great anxiety over the destiny of that child, which had cost me much labor and travail for six years to bring it forth; and as it is a great favorite of mine, I hope it will grow to a glorious perfection, and that its benign influence throughout the state may be felt amongst all orders, especially the poor; for which it was principally projected."[19]

The matter of the distribution of the school funds was settled by the legislation of 1813. At this time Clinton was presiding officer of the Senate, and it is difficult to indicate just what form his influence took, and to what extent he exercised any influence at all. The only piece of evidence bearing directly on this particular case is a letter from Divie Bethune, which is quoted below. It also indicates the attitude of the Trustees of the Free School Society toward Clinton—and thus reinforces some points indicated above.

NEW YORK, Feb. 26, 1812.

THE HON. DE WITT CLINTON,

DEAR SIR:

The deep solicitude I feel for the welfare of the New York Free School Society, must plead my excuse for thus intruding on your time. Mr. Buckley has informed you of the appointment of himself, and W. De Peyster, on the special mission recommended by you. The crisis is important to the future prosperity of the school, and probably decisive as to the extent of a system, which liberally endowed, might prove a blessing, and a glory to our state, if not to the United States. Sensibly impressed with the propriety of improving the present moment, I have ventured on the throwing in my mite of exertion, however small, into the general stock.

Having lately received Joseph Lancaster's report of his commencement, progress, and success from 1798 to 1811, I have made interesting extracts, accompanied by a few reflections, tending to enlist the popular feeling in favor of our Valuable Institu-

---

[19]L. to C., v. 4, p. 56.

tion, in the disposition of the school fund, without adverting to the latter in direct terms. I have given them to Mr. Lang (his paper being less occupied by political matter), and expect they will appear in his *Gazette* on Friday, or Saturday. If you should judge these extracts and remarks calculated to produce a good effect, you could have them copied into one of the Albany papers, and thus bring them home to the desk of each member of the Legislature.

Another measure has suggested itself to my mind this evening, and is the immediate cause of my addressing you. It is this, and one which, I think, could be completely accomplished; to draw up a short, concise, and expressive Petition to the Legislature, requesting them to place the proportion of the School Fund for this city, under the direction of the New York Free School Society. I have no doubt but a goodly number of respectable men, of every denomination in the midst of us, would cheerfully sign such a petition.

This would create a united and powerful interest in our favor; would hardly leave any excitement for, and many obstacles against any one religious denomination undertaking the unpopular, and unpropitious task of opposing us with any proper position of animation, or prospect of success.

I am induced to submit this plan to your consideration immediately, as your sanction of it would strengthen the disposition and exertions of our trustees to carry it into effect. I have not had an opportunity of sounding one of them since I thought of it, but shall to-morrow. If you should recommend such a measure, you will be able to have postponed the ultimate decision of the Legislature, until a general petition should be executed and sent up.

Your answer, should you favor me with one, shall be communicated to the trustees.

I am with much respect,
Dear Sir,
DIVIE BETHUNE.[20]

The legislation of 1813 was decisive, for it provided the basis of a permanent means of support.

During Clinton's life two more laws were passed, the law of April 5, 1817, and that of January 28, 1826. The former, "An act respecting the Free School Society of New York,"[21] provided in section one that a number of additional trustees not exceeding twelve may be appointed. The second section follows:

---

[20]L. to C., v. 5, p. 4.
[21]Chap. 145, Laws of 1817.

"And be it further enacted that if any surplus school money shall remain in the hands of the trustees after an ample compensation to the teachers employed by them, it shall and may be lawful to apply such surplus to the instruction of school masters on the Lancasterian plan, to the erection of buildings for schools, and to all the needful purposes of a common school education and to no other purpose whatever."

The remainder of the act points out that on Manhattan Island and two adjacent settlements, about one thousand children are destitute of the means of education, that a lot has been appropriated, and that with a sum of money out of the excise fund raised in the said city as has been done on similar and former occasions, the trustees will be enabled with their other resources to dispense the blessings of education in that quarter of the city. It, therefore, provided for the payment to the Trustees of the Free School Society of two thousand dollars for the exclusive purpose of erecting a suitable building.

The act of 1826[22] provided for a change of the name of the society to the "Public School Society of New York." It was further enacted that it shall be the duty of said society to provide, as far as in their means, for the education of all children in the City of New York not otherwise provided for; whether such children be or be not the proper objects of a gratuitous education and without regard to the religious sect or denomination to which such children or their parents belong.

Another important provision[23] is the one permitting the trustees "to charge a moderate compensation adapted to the ability of the parents, to be applied to the erection of school houses, the payment of teachers' salaries, and to such other expenses as may be incident to the education of children. Provided that such payment or compensation may be remitted by the trustees, in all cases in which they shall deem it proper to do so. And, provided, further, that no child shall be denied the benefits of the said institution, merely on the ground of inability to pay for the same, but shall at all times be freely received and educated by the said trustees."

The fourth section is as follows: "That nothing in this act shall be construed to deprive the said society of any revenues or of any rights to which they are now, or if this

---

[22]Chap. 25, Laws of 1826.
[23]Sec. 3.

act had not been passed, would have been entitled, and that the receipts of small payments from the scholars shall not preclude the trustees from drawing from the Common School Fund for all the children educated by them." The other provisions with the exception of the last, provides for minor matters: amount of subscription to become a member; increase in number of trustees; times of meeting, etc. The last section provides for a step in the direction in which things were moving. It was further enacted: "That the said society is hereby authorized to convey their school edifices to the Mayor, aldermen and commonalty of the City of New York upon such terms and conditions and in such form as shall be agreed upon between the parties, taking back from the said corporation a perpetual lease thereof upon condition that the same shall be exclusively and perpetually applied to the purpose of education."

In conclusion we may see what an examination of the books of minutes reveals as to Clinton's connection with the society. The written volumes of minutes in the possession of the New York Historical Society begin with the second volume, and the first minute is for the annual meeting of 1817 under date of May 5. The first volume is unfortunately lost—at least it is not to be found among the Public School Society papers, now in the possession of the Historical Society.

Clinton was present at the special meeting held May 19, 1817, to take measures for building a school house in the neighborhood of Manhattan Island.[24] A committee was elected with Thomas Eddy as chairman.

The next meeting that Clinton attended was held December 4, 1818. We find the following minute under this date: "On motion of the President it was resolved that Joseph Lancaster be permitted to use the school rooms of this society at such times as shall not interfere with school hours, for the purpose of delivering lectures on the system of education invented by him."[25]

At the annual meeting of May 7, 1824, Clinton was re-elected president as usual. We find also this minute: "The society having been informed that at the request of the Board of Trustees the Honorable De Witt Clinton, the President of the Society, is

[24]Cf. Chap. 145, Laws of 1817.
[25]Minutes of the Public School Society, v. 2, under date given (Ms.).

engaged in writing a history of the society from its commencement, and which is nearly ready for the press, it was 'Resolved,
That said History be printed and distributed under the direction
of the trustees.' "[26]

The next important reference to Clinton during his life is
found under date of November 11, 1825. This was a special
meeting called after public notice. De Witt Clinton was present
and presided. The following significant resolution was passed:

"Resolved, That this society approve of the plan proposed in the
report of the Committee of the Trustees in relation to the changes
of the Free School Society into a Public School Society and the
trustees are hereby authorized to take such measures to carry the
said plan into effect as they deem proper."

By another resolution the trustees were authorized to apply to
the Legislature for such alterations in their act of incorporation
as they may deem proper.[27]

Summary. The significance of the Public School Society lay
in these facts: First, during a period when the necessity of the
social control of education was not clearly seen nor adequately
felt by Society, this society provided educational opportunities
for the children of the city. Secondly, this society educated public opinion to the point where it saw clearly its duty as to the social
control of education, and acted on its conception of its duty.
Thirdly, this society organized and developed a fairly adequate
machinery for carrying on the work of education. Finally, this
society perceived clearly the necessity for well informed and well
trained teachers, if the social results—yes, and the individual
results—were to be at all realized, and it provided means (from
our standpoint, of course, rudimental) for the professional training of teachers.

Nor was the society of merely local significance; its influence
was state-wide and even national. This influence will be shown
in detail in the discussion of the Lancasterian system and the
training of teachers.

It may be safely said that without Clinton the Public School
Society would have been impotent to do its great work. It was

---

[26] I have found no trace of this "History."
[27] Cf. Clinton's message for 1826 and Chap. 25, Laws of 1826.

Clinton who introduced and secured the passage of the act of incorporation, and the successive acts modifying the act of incorporation to meet the changed conceptions of the society's work and the consequent changed needs. Whenever any questions affecting the Public School Society were before the Legislature, Clinton invariably looked after its interests and they were protected. As Mayor of New York City, and consequently a member of the Common Council, Clinton was as ever the zealous guardian of the interests of the society.

Important as was the conception and organization of the society, the financial support conditioned both and made the continuance of the society possible. This financial support was provided for by means of ward collections, subscriptions, grants of the Common Council of New York City, special legislative grants and the general act of 1813, besides the membership fees, which were comparatively insignificant. Clinton paid his membership fees, made a collection in the first ward, and contributed generously besides. He was instrumental—as already indicated in detail—in securing the special legislative grants and his influence was not lacking in securing the Common Council grants. Though the record of the legislation of 1813 does not bear on the face of it the evidence of Clinton's agency in securing its passage, we know, nevertheless, from other sources his vital connection with it.

One other contribution Clinton made to this society, namely, his own services. During a quarter of a century, i.e., from the inception of the society in 1805 to his death in 1828, Clinton was president of the society. Until his first term as Governor (1817) he was actively in charge of its affairs and presided at its meetings, but thereafter while annually re-elected to the presidency, he presided only at extraordinary meetings. However, he continued to keep in touch with the affairs of the society.

The Minor School Societies

The work of the Public School Society was supplemented by the work of several minor societies, which provided educational opportunities for certain special groups of children. These were the Economical School Society, the Orphan School Society, and the Infant School Society. Clinton's influence was as manifest in these minor societies as in the main one.

The Economical School Society. The first of the lesser school societies to be discussed is the Economical School Society. The purpose of this society is indicated in detail in the report made by Clinton which is given below in full.

A. Hyde Neuville addressed to Clinton on April 11, 1809, the following letter:

"I have the honor of addressing you on the plan of a liberal institution. You are so well known to be the zealous protector of all establishments of this kind, that I believe myself sufficiently authorized in claiming in favor of this one, your benevolent interest.

"Deign, Sir, to place your name first on the list of actual members of the society—it will assure the success of this institution."[28]

The Economical School Society secured during the following year favorable legislative action. On February 20, 1810, the trustees and members of the Economical School Society prayed the Legislature to grant "such aid as in their wisdom shall be deemed proper." The petition was read and referred to a select committee consisting of Messrs. Clinton, Selden, and Bartow. On March 6, Clinton reported as follows:

"That the said institution was originally founded for the education of poor persons driven by the unfortunate events of war in foreign parts; that it has since been extended to the indigent of all nationalities; that it is formed on the celebrated plan of Lancaster; contains upward of 200 scholars; is calculated to be eminently useful, and is supported principally by the founders. It is, therefore, the opinion of the committee that it is justly entitled to the favorable notice of the State."[29]

Leave was asked to bring in a bill granting the prayer of the petitioners, which was granted. The bill was read a first time and, by unanimous consent, a second time, and referred to a committee of the whole. On March 7, it was reported amended and ordered engrossed. It passed the Senate the next day.

On March 1, 1812, A. Hyde Neuville addressed "To the Hon. De Witt Clinton, President of the Senate," the following letter:

---

[28]L. to C., v. 4, p. 48.
[29]*Senate Journal*, March 6, 1810.

"SIR:

"I have the honor of addressing to you the petition of the trustees of the Economical School who are so fortunate as to reckon you one of their members.

"A year ago you were so good as to promise me your assistance for this year—I presume, therefore, to observe to you that the building we have constructed will oblige us to loan the sum of about $1,200—and if we could obtain the assistance of the State[30] our establishment would be in a flourishing situation and we should not be obliged to importunate the Legislature.

"Deign to accept, Sir, the homage of my respect and high consideration."

We find this plea of M. Neuville answered in Chapter 52 of the Laws of 1813: "An act supplementary to an act entitled An act for the establishment of common schools," which extended the provision of the latter act to the City and County of New York. It "authorized, empowered and required the Mayor, Recorder and Aldermen of the City of New York, to raise and collect a tax on the inhabitants of the said city equal to the amount which shall be apportioned by the State." It provided, further, that this money should be distributed and paid to the Trustees of the Free School Society, the Orphan Asylum Society, the Society of the Economical School, the African Free School, and such incorporated religious societies, which now support or hereafter shall establish charity schools within the said city, as may apply for same, "provided, however, in every case that the session is at least of nine months duration."

Clinton later became president of the society. This fact appears indirectly from a letter written by Clinton as directed in a resolution passed unanimously "by a meeting of the Trustees of the Economical School of New York on the 19th of May, 1814." The resolution recites the fact that A. Hyde de Neuville, the organizer, a Trustee and Secretary of the Society, who is about to resign, has unremittingly and with a liberal appropriation of his time, talent and money devoted himself to the school—by which means it (the school) has arrived at such flourishing state, that it now dispenses the blessings of education to several hundred children—it was resolved that the President signify the high sense of appreciation of the Board of Trustees. This he did in a letter dated from New York on the same day.

---

[30]Part of the Common School Fund.

The last reference found is contained in a Report of a Committee of the Trustees of the Free School Society on the Distribution of the Common School Fund, dated at New York, January 28, 1825. The report says: "Of these 10,383 children, 6,976 were educated in the schools of the Free School Society, the African Free School Society, the Female Association, the Mechanics Society, the Hamilton Free School, the Orphan Asylum and the Economical School, and the remaining 3,407 attended the various sectarian or church schools." The report contains a plan for the distribution of the fund, and no provision is made for the Economical School Society which had already become a part of the Public School Society and hence no separate provision was necessary. The report proposed that the Female Association and the African School Society should likewise become an integral part of the Free School Society. For the Economical School Society this union with the latter was a perfectly natural result, with Clinton as its president and with aims identical with those of the Free School Society.

The Orphan Asylum Society. Another of the minor societies in which Clinton's influence was felt is the Orphan Asylum Society. The principal facts in connection with this society may be briefly given. The society was incorporated April 7, 1807, and Clinton was instrumental in securing the incorporation. This society was included in the distribution of the school funds provided by chapter 52 of the laws of 1813. In the first controversy with the religious societies, when the distribution of the fund was left to the Common Council (1825), the Orphan Asylum Society was continued as a beneficiary. In the second controversy the Roman Catholic Benevolent Society, in behalf of its Orphan Asylum, claimed to be entitled to part of the fund on the same ground as was the Orphan Asylum. It was then (1831) decided that this claim was "in full accordance with the cardinal principles of the ordinance of 1825 recognizing the peculiar claims of the orphan asylum as a justifiable and the only justifiable exception to the general principle that the Public School moneys were applicable only to secular instruction."[31]

---

[31]Randall's History of the Common School System of the State of New York, p. 76.

Clinton's influence on this society may be best indicated by the following two letters. The first is quoted in full:

"NEW YORK, April 16, 1808.

"DEAR SIR:

"I have just had the honor of receiving you polite letter inclosing extracts from the acts of the Legislature.

"We are sensible, however, that any feeble testimony of gratitude we can render, will be a slight compensation to the applause of your heart, and we pray and trust that both will be infinitely exceeded by the blessing which heaven has peculiarly promised for the charitable.

"With respect and esteem, I have the honor to be

"Your most humble servant,

"SARAH HOFFMAN."

"To HON. DE WITT CLINTON."[32]

The other letter is from the secretary of the society, and opens somewhat as the preceding closes. She says in part: "These general reflections are roused by your (Clinton's) well timed exertions in the presentation of their late petition to the Legislature." She goes on to say:

"Therefore, I am directed to express these sentiments to you, Sir, and through you, to all those gentlemen who concurred with you in obtaining the liberal grant of 500 dollars per annum for this institution. And with sincere wishes for your prosperity and private happiness,

"I have the honor, Sir, to subscribe myself in their name, your most obedient, humble servant,

"MARY STANSBERY, *Secretary.*"

"New York, April 17, 1811."[33]

The Infant School Society. Clinton was interested in all fields of education, in elementary, secondary and advanced. He was interested, too, in what would now be called the kindergarten stage. However, Clinton's inspiration came from England—the home of the infant school movement. In Clinton's Letter Books, we find the following letter:[34]

"ALBANY, 21, Jan., 1825.

"MY WORTHY FRIEND,

"I thank you for your kind letter containing an outline of the Infantile Schools of London. These establishments possess merit

---

[32]L. to C., v. 4, p. 27.
[33]L. to C., v. 4, p. 78.
[34]V. 6, p. 380.

and if the execution is only equal to the plan they must achieve a wonderful revolution. I have written a friend in New York urging their introduction into that city."

In his message to the Legislature the following year we find this statement: "In early infancy education must be usefully administered. In some parts of Great Britain infant schools have been successfully established, comprising children from two to six years of age whose tempers, hearts and minds are ameliorated, and whose indigent parents are enabled by this means to devote themselves to labor without interruption or uneasiness. Institutions of this kind are adapted only to a dense population and must be left to the guardianship of private benevolence."

Another letter dated Albany, January 9, 1827, shows Clinton's evident pleasure at the success of the efforts to establish an infant school society. It reads:

"Madam:

"Your letter of the fifth afforded me great pleasure. I now feel assured that the establishment of Infant Schools, a plan which has long been a favorite of mine, will at length succeed in such hands as is proposed. There can be no doubt of the realization of all the anticipated blessings.

"I beg leave to offer you and your associates, the expression of my high sense of the benevolence, public spirit and good sense which mark the undertaking and so assure you that my best services will be at your command."[35]

Another valuable letter dated from Albany, 7th Oct., 1827, follows:

"Madam:

"I had the honor of receiving your interesting communication relative to the Infant Society of the City of New York. I rejoice that this excellent establishment is under such able direction. I will certainly visit it as soon as I reach the City. Its prosperity lies near my heart and will always command my best exertions.

"I enclose checque for 15 dollars to constitute me a member for life."[36]

The first meeting of what was to be the Infant School Society was held May 23, 1827. The fourth meeting was held on June 28, 1827, "at which a constitution was adopted, officers and manager were chosen and a letter was read from his Excellency

---

[35]L. B., v. 8, p. 141.
[36]L. B., v. 8, Oct. 7, 1827.

De Witt Clinton, Governor of the State, who consented to become the patron of the Society, which in fact was organized at his suggestion."[37]

In the message to the Legislature the following year (1828) Clinton wrote:

"The institution of infant schools is the pedestal to the pyramid. It embraces those children who are generally too young for common schools; it relieves parents from engrossed attention to their offspring, softens the brow of care and lightens the hand of labor. More efficacious in reaching the heart than the head, in improving the temper than the intellect, it has been eminently useful in laying the foundation of good feelings, good principles and good habits."[38]

In May, 1827, the Infant School Society secured permission to use the basement rooms of School No. 8, and several months later received similar permission for No. 10. Women were employed as teachers. The Public School Society soon took control of the work in conjunction with the ladies of the Infant School Society. After the full adoption of the Infant School System in 1830, there was no reason for the separate existence of the Infant School Society.

Summary. Clinton was instrumental—and largely so—in securing acts of incorporation for the Manumission Society (the African Free School), Economical School Society and the Orphan Asylum Society. Knowing as we do that Clinton played an important part in securing the legislation providing for the Common School Fund, we may be sure that these three societies were included in the distribution of the fund along with the Public School Society through Clinton's instrumentality; in the case of the Economical School Society, this is clear. He was largely responsible, too, in securing in 1811, the grant of five hundred dollars annually for the Orphan Asylum Society. The distribution of the Common School Fund made the further appeal of these societies to the Legislature unnecessary.

Clinton had been interested in infants' schools several years before the organization of the Infant School Society. He sug-

---

[37]Bourne, p. 659.

[38]The following year the Female Association conducted infant schools instead of girls' schools.

gested the organization of the society, encouraged it at the beginning by letter and by becoming its patron, became a life member and noticed it favorably in his last message to the Legislature.

The Training of Teachers

Clinton's thought, here as elsewhere, was far in advance of his time. No community under the circumstances could have adopted his suggestions. Nevertheless it was a great service to keep before the minds of the people and the Legislature the importance, necessity and duty of providing for adequately trained teachers, not merely through the initiative of the prospective teacher nor through the agency of privately endowed and administered institutions, but in public schools set apart for this sole purpose. Nowhere in the United States at this time was there such an institution nor was there to be any until 1839. Clinton's contribution here was twofold. He impressed upon his generation the necessity for professionally trained teachers, but more than that he emphasized the amazing doctrine for the time that the provision of such teachers was an imperative social duty. The result of this public discussion and agitation together with Clinton's private efforts was fourfold: (1) the passage of the law of 1827, and ultimately, with additional forces at work, the laws of 1834 and 1844; (2) the incorporation of the Society of Teachers; (3) the Public School Society's efforts in training teachers; and (4) the training given under the direction of various Lancasterian societies.

State Legislation. "It is clear, therefore," says B. A. Hinsdale after indicating the conditions, "that at the opening of the century there was an urgent need of a general educational revival throughout the country, and particularly of a revival or creation of interest in the training of teachers." It is almost needless to say that it must be a creation. In the next paragraph we find this statement: "In America, as in Europe, the demand for better teachers was a marked feature of the great democratic movement toward education; perhaps it may be called the feature of this movement."[39]

The connection between the democratic movement of education and trained teachers was clearly perceived by Clinton and

---

[39]Hinsdale, Horace Mann, p. 9.

found adequate and repeated expression as noted in Chapter II. In general his argument took this form: The general enlightenment of the people is absolutely essential to the protection, preservation, and perpetuation of our republican form of government To what kind of people is this great work entrusted? Clinton's own question is more significant: "Ought the mind and the morals of the rising and perhaps the destinies of all future generations to be entrusted to the guardianship of incompetence?" There then follows in successive messages his series of recommendations: "I, therefore, recommend a seminary for the education of teachers in the monitorial system of instruction." (1826) In 1827 we have his commendation of what was being done by the New York Public School Society and certain public-spirited citizens in Livingston County, and his recommendations of a "central school in each county for the education of teachers and other momentous purposes connected with the improvement of the human mind." Less than two months before his death, we find his county monitorial high school recommendation, "a measure so well calculated to raise the character of our schoolmasters and to double the power of our artizans by giving them a scientific education." (1828)

In 1821 the Board of Regents, of which Clinton was one, speaking of the academies says that "it is to these seminaries that we must look for a supply of teachers for the common school." The committee to whom was referred that portion of the Governor's message referring to the education of teachers was of a similar opinion. The report prepared by the chairman, John C. Spencer, says: "But in the view which the committee have taken, our great reliance for nurseries of teachers must be placed in our colleges and academies. In connection with these the committee admit that the establishment of a separate institution for the sole purpose of preparing teachers would be a most valuable auxiliary." But as yet no legislative action whatever had been taken.

The first law on the subject was passed April 13, 1827. This was "An act to provide permanent funds for the annual appropriation to common schools, to increase the literature fund and *to promote the education of teachers.*"[40] No further reference

_____

[40]Chap. 228, Laws of 1827. The italics are ours.

is made to the subject, that is, the bill proper contains no reference to it. The increase of the Literature Fund, by providing
increased amounts of money for the academies and the changed
basis for the distribution of the money, by requiring increased
scholarship in higher branches of education than heretofore, was
intended as the means for promoting the education of teachers.
In the 1828 Report of the Regents we find the statement:
"The academies have become, in the opinion of the Regents, what
it has always been desirable they should be, fit Seminaries for imparting instruction in the higher branches of English education
and especially for qualifying teachers of Common Schools."[41]
Soon, therefore, beginning with Canandaigua and St. Lawrence
Academies in 1831, in the reports of the academies we find "Principles of Teaching," as a special study. Clinton's recommendation of a seminary for the education of teachers was not carried
out in New York State until 1844. The logical outcome of his
last three messages was the famous law of May 2, 1834[42]—"the
first law passed in New York and indeed in this country, making
provision for the education of teachers for common schools."[43]
The first section of this act provides that revenue may be distributed by the Regents of the University to the academies subject
to their visitation. Section two reads:

"The trustees of academies to which any distribution of
money shall be made by virtue of this act shall cause the same
to be expended in educating teachers of common schools in such
manner and under such regulation as said regents shall prescribe."

This—the first form of the normal school idea in the United States
if we except the Lancasterian attempts—continued in force as the
only system of training teachers, until the establishment, by the
law of May 7, 1844, of the Albany Normal School.

Summary. Clinton's influence in this connection is not easily
nor exactly measurable. Probably his most important service
was bringing definitely to social self-consciousness the need of professionally trained, or, at least, more adequately trained teachers,
and its connection with the very foundation of the social structure.
It, however, did not remain merely an idea. As a direct result

---

[41]Hough's Historical and Statistical Record, p. 528.
[42]Chap. 241, Laws of 1834.
[43]Gordy's Rise and Growth of the Normal School Idea in the United States,
p. 31.

of the 1827 message, though the legislative committee was not willing to go as far as Clinton was, we have the law of 1827—the first on the subject. The more adequate response to Clinton's efforts is the academy movement in the training of teachers—which the law of 1827 really initiated. The ultimate response was the law establishing the State Normal School at Albany (1844). Had Clinton lived longer there can be little doubt that the movement would have been greatly accelerated.

The Society of Teachers

On February 4, 1811, George Ironside sent to Clinton, with his permission, the petition and bill of the Society of Teachers.[44] This petition was received by the Senate and read March 4, 1811. Clinton, on this day introduced "An act to incorporate the Society of Teachers in the City of New York for benevolent and literary purposes." On the same day it was read twice and referred to a committee of the whole. This committee made an amendment and on March 25, it was read a third time and passed. It passed the Assembly on April 4 and the Council of Revision on the 5th.

This act made the society a "body corporate and politic," thereby granting them the usual privileges of a corporation. The act was to be operative for a period of fifteen years. The aim or purpose of the society may be definitely indicated from the preamble to its constitution. The men interested in the movement "formed themselves into a society or organization for the relief and benefit of decayed teachers and their families, the widows and children of deceased teachers, and for the discussion of literary subjects and the promotion of science among the members of the society under the name and title of 'The Society of Teachers of the City of New York for Benevolent and Literary Purposes.' "[45] Apparently the society was not organized under the act of 1811, for during the first year of Clinton's first term as Governor (April, 1818) he approved a bill entitled "An act to revive an act entitled 'An act to incorporate the Society of Teachers in the City of New York for benevolent and literary purposes.' "

The detailed statement of the society's aims prepared by a committee[46] and intended for publication appeared in the *Academi-*

---

[44]L. to C., v. 4, p. 65.
[45]Laws of 1818, p. 137.
[46]Messrs. Picket and Payne.

cian of October, 1818. Besides the importance of the statement with reference to the professional training of teachers it throws interesting side-lights on the social status of the teacher. It is said that the improvements which every day appear "have created the necessity for an association of professional men by whom the improvements may be tested, embodied and carried out in a practical application."

The report further points out that there are two ways of benefiting teaching: the one by developing principles and accompanying them with lucid demonstration both as to what they are and their relations, and the other by following out the practical application of these principles and applying "to them those mechanical facilities which fit them for the business of teaching." The purpose of the society was to embody into a system the excellences of each and to add "whatever the intelligence and observation of American instructors may furnish."

The purposes of the society as stated were to secure grading of the schools, the establishment of a high school, and owing to the "precarious nature" of the business to provide for those who otherwise would "drag out their old age in indigence."

Finally, it was the purpose of the society to "vindicate to ourselves the name and character of a liberal profession." That this was a difficult proposition was clearly recognized by these men. The report says: "The consideration in which his labors (the teacher's) are generally held is far below their intrinsic dignity and the station they have to claim from their usefulness to society." The committee express the hope that the time is not far distant "when the instructors of youth shall be welcome as brethren by the members of the liberal professions." And a final quotation: "There is nothing then in the nature of the duties of an instructor which can disqualify him for occupying an equal rank with men of the other liberal professions."

Summary. There is very little existent material bearing on the doings of this society. One significant fact for us, however, is that a body of men with such fine professional aspirations looked up to Clinton as their champion. Clinton made the existence of the Society possible through his securing for it the act of incorporation. It was probably Clinton's influence, too, which secured the revival of the act during his first term as Governor.

Free School Society's Training of Teachers

In the Ninth Annual Report we find this statement: "From the commencement of the society it has been an object of great interest to train up young men for the office of teachers in similar institutions. The realization of their wishes in this respect is in part accomplished." A youth educated in the Chatham Street school was at this time superintending a similar school in New Brunswick, New Jersey, and an application had come to fill the vacancy in Newburg, New York.

The 1815 report indicates the places where the Lancasterian system was introduced. The eleventh report (1816) records the fact that the school at New Brunswick is being "conducted with great propriety." It also says that the "benefits derived from the Lancasterian system of instruction will very soon be made generally known and enjoyed in the United States." The means of bringing this about is indicated in the fourteenth report (1819): "With a deep solicitude for diffusing the means of education among the poor and for the general extension of the Lancasterian system throughout the country the Trustees invite all those persons who are desirous of obtaining a knowledge of this method of instruction to repair to the schools under their charge, where in the space of six or eight weeks a competent knowledge of the Lancasterian method of instruction can be obtained without fee or reward." The invitation is repeated in the report of 1820.

The further development of this movement is best indicated in connection with the progress of the Lancasterian movement and will be found in the next section.

The Lancasterian System

The point of departure here may well be the statement of the Lancasterian system contained in Clinton's address at the opening of the first school of the Free School Society, December 11, 1809. The first part of the address referring to Lancaster and the Lancasterian system opens with this sentence: "In the year 1798 an obscure man by the name of Joseph Lancaster, possessed of an original genius and a sagacious mind, and animated by a sublime benevolence, devoted himself to the education of the poor of Great Britain." Clinton proceeds to give a general exposition of the system and refers to Lancaster's "Improvements in Education" for a more detailed account. After referring to Lancaster's work in England—paying special attention to the Borough Road school—he also says:

"When I perceive that many boys in our school have been taught to read and write in two months, who did not before know the alphabet, and that even one has accomplished it in three weeks—when I view all the bearings and tendencies of this system—when I contemplate the habits of order which it forms, the spirit of emulation which it excites, the rapid improvement which it produces, the purity of morals which it inculcates—when I behold the extraordinary union of celerity in instruction and economy in expense—and when I perceive one great assembly of a thousand children, under the eye of a single teacher, marching, with unexampled rapidity and with perfect discipline, to the goal of knowledge, *I confess that I recognize in Lancaster the benefactor of the human race. I consider his system as creating a new era in education, as a blessing sent down from heaven to redeem the poor and distressed of the world from the power and dominion of ignorance.*"[47]

The address later points out that the system had already been extended to the charity schools of the Dutch, Episcopalian, and Methodist Churches and to the Presbyterian School in Rutgers Street and to the school of the Manumission Society. Two deputations had visited the school and made highly favorable reports. As a result of one of these, the Adelphia Society (Philadelphia) was organized, which soon erected a handsome two-story building and adopted the Lancasterian system. The other deputation was from the Philadelphia Free School Society, which, as a result of the report of the deputation, adopted the system where it "flourishes beyond expectation." Two female schools, the Aimwell School in Philadelphia, and another in Burlington, New Jersey, had also embraced the plan "with equal success."

We find in the reports of the society that the system was later extended to the female schools of the city, the schools of the Orphan Asylum and the Economical School. In the tenth annual report (1815) we find a summary statement "that schools in this improved method of tuition, have been established in Philadelphia, Baltimore, Georgetown, Albany, Hartford and New Brunswick," and similar schools on a smaller scale in Burlington and Mount Holly, New Jersey, and at Flushing, Long Island.

---

[47]Bourne, p. 19. The italics are ours.

The spread of the system was a distinct purpose of the trustees of the Free School Society. It was avowed by Clinton in his 1809 address. It was definitely avowed by the trustees in 1819, and the training of teachers was one phase of it.

Requests for teachers frequently came to Clinton as president of the Free School Society. The following letter is a typical instance of Clinton's recommendation:

"ALBANY, 3d March, 1816.

"GENTLEMEN:

"I have the pleasure of introducing to you Mr. E. Baker, whom I have heretofore recommended to you and I confidently hope that such an arrangement will be made as will confer all the benefits of this invaluable system of your village which I have no doubt will be fully effected by employing him."[48]

The following is a detailed statement of the progress of the Lancasterian movement in New York State.[49] We have already noted that Clinton was instrumental in securing permission for Lancaster to use the rooms of the Free School Society for lecturing when they were not being used for purposes of instruction. Lancaster's further progress in the State is indicated in the following letter to Clinton:

"WATERFORD, 9 mo. 11th, 1818.

"HONORED FRIEND:

"My lecture at Troy was crowned with all the anticipated success. The president and trustees waited on me in a body and we walked together to the Lecture Room. About 200 persons attended—the receipts about $48—the expense little except our carriage and advertisements which were only a trifle. The lectures at New York, Albany, Troy, and Waterford established a kind of criterion by which I may expect that the produce of lecturing will be likely to clear all the travelling expenses attending it.

"The lecture here was numerously attended. I shall leave the bearer, my kind and hospitable friend, Mr. Morgan, to report.

"I feel deeply indebted to thy kind attention for much of the hospitality I have received at Troy. I slept at the house of General Thomas—my own fellow professors behaved with kind and brotherly attention. I am to visit the school at Troy to-day by ap-

[48]L. B., v. 2, p. 279.
[49]The historian of the Lancasterian movement in the United States and in South America will find exceedingly valuable information in the volumes containing the letters to Clinton. See v. 8, pp. 20, 54, 56, 58 ; v. 9, pp. 5, 11, 16, 20 ; v. 11, pp. 30, 34 ; v. 12, p. 5 ; v. 14, pp. 14, 32, 51.

pointment at three o'clock. I am also invited to lecture at Lansingburgh which invitation I shall accept for the sake of being near my friends on the first day.

"The City of Hudson is now a place where I should make some arrangements prior to their papers being published. The favor of a line from thyself introducing me to some person there will be acceptable and may be addressed to me at Albany, as soon as leisure admits. I should be glad to lecture at Hudson about the 19th or 20th on my way to New York visiting Schenectady in the interim.

"I remain with much respect,
"Thy obliged friend,
"JOSEPH LANCASTER."

"To GOVERNOR DE WITT CLINTON."[50]

State legislation gives further details as to the progress of the movement. The commissioners appointed by the Governor pursuant to the act of April 9, 1811, to report a system for the organization and establishment of common schools and for the distribution of the Common School Fund, applied to the Trustees of the Free School Society, through Clinton, for information as to the Lancasterian system. The information was supplied. In the report we find the following paragraph:

"As to the particular mode of instruction best calculated to communicate to the young mind the greatest quantity of useful knowledge in a given time, and with the least expense, the commissioners beg leave to observe that there are a variety of new methods lately adopted, in various parts of Europe, of imparting instruction to youths, some of which methods have been partially introduced into the United States. The Lancasterian plan, as it is called which has been recently introduced in some of the large towns of the United States, merits the serious consideration of the Legislature. As an expeditious and cheap mode of instructing a large number of scholars, it stands unrivaled, and the certificates of the Trustees of the New York Free School, together with those of diverse tutors, carry with them the evidence of its vast utility and success. The commissioners, therefore, recommend that a number of Lancaster's books, containing an account of his teaching, etc., be printed by order of the Legislature and distributed among the several towns of this state."[51]

The progress of the movement outside of New York City is most conveniently indicated by the organization of Lancaster

[50]L. to C., v. 8, p. 56.
[51]Randall, p. 21.

school societies. The "Albany Lancaster School Society" was incorporated May 26, 1812.[52] The school organized by the society later became a city institution. In 1816 a Schenectady Lancaster School Society was authorized and continued in existence for a quarter of a century.[53] The Catskill Lancaster School Society" was incorporated by the act of March 14, 1817,[54] and abolished by an act of April 20, 1830: (Chap. 284). By an act of April 15, 1817,[55] a number of men of Hudson incorporated into a society for the establishment of a Lancasterian school which continued in existence long after Clinton's death. And finally the "Monitorial School Society," in the village of Lansingburgh was incorporated April 14, 1827.[56] The next year Clinton died and it is significant that no more Lancasterian school societies were organized.

SECONDARY EDUCATION

By the opening of the nineteenth century, the system of secondary education in New York State had been fairly well established and its details well organized. There was little opportunity in this field and consequently it is here that Clinton's influence on education was least felt. His connection with secondary education may be briefly stated. He was Secretary of the Board of Regents from 1794 to 1797 and was elected Regent in 1808 and continued as such until his death. He visited academies and reported on their work, and took a prominent part in the promotion of medical education, as will be noted later.

Another phase of this movement which attracted Clinton's attention, probably to a greater extent that we can now trace, is the high school movement. The men identified with this movement were Clinton's personal friends who had worked with him in several of the philanthropic-educational movements previously discussed. The leader of this movement was John Griscom, who travelled extensively in Europe, noting especially the monitorial high schools in Scotland, and who embodied his experience in a noteworthy book "A Year in Europe." It was Clinton who supplied him with the introductions to the prominent people in Europe

---

[52]Chap. 55, Laws of 1812.
[53]Hough, p. 430.
[54]Chap. 87, Laws of 1817.
[55]Chap. 272, Laws of 1817.
[56]Chap. 272, Laws of 1827.

whom he met. Under these circumstances it is a safe inference that Clinton was consulted in the planning and organization of the High School Society. This inference becomes a certainty—at least a probability—when considered in connection with certain other facts. The High School Society proposed establishing monitorial high schools—a favorite idea of Clinton's. In the first report of this society (1824), and thereafter, Clinton's name is found among the stockholders. The society was incorporated the following year (1825) when Clinton became Governor.

The great immediate problem in secondary education was to secure adequate funds to support the system. This was accomplished at the time by means of the Literature Fund. The first step in this direction was taken in 1790 when the Legislature authorized the Regents to lease out certain land and apply the rents and profits to aid the academies and colleges of the state. It will be noticed that this provided for no capital, and hence it missed its opportunity.

This was remedied by the act of 1813. An act passed April 12,[57] directed that the Crumhorn Mountain tract be sold for the benefit of academies as the Regents of the University might direct. It was sold and $10,416 capital was thereby added to the Literature Fund. The next day there was passed "An act to authorize the sale of lands appropriated for the promotion of literature."[58] By this act the commissioners of the Land Office were required to sell all the land formerly granted for the promotion of literature, in the Military tract, and in Chenango and Broome counties, and to invest the proceeds as best calculated to secure the principal and interest. From a report made in 1818, it appears that funds amounting to $29,735.09 were derived from the sale of these lands.

Evidence is wanting as to Clinton's direct connections with these laws. However, we know that he was actively interested in the distribution of the Common School Fund during these very years, and it is not unlikely that these bills received some of his attention and assistance.

The two succeeding laws on the subject were passed during

---

[57] Chap. 187, Laws of 1813.
[58] Chap. 191, Laws of 1813.

Clinton's first and last terms as Governor.   In 1819[59] the arrears
of quit rents were divided equally between the Literature and
Common School Funds.   In 1827[60] securities of the Canal Fund,
amounting to $150,000, were transferred to the Literature Fund.
The income from the total fund under control of the Regents,
including this addition, was to be distributed to the incorporated
academies and seminaries, not colleges, which were under the
control of the Regents, or that might place themselves under their
control, on the basis of the number of pupils instructed during the
preceding year, who had pursued classical studies or the higher
branches of an English education, or both.

[59]Chap. 222, Laws of 1819.
[60]Chap. 225, Laws of 1827.

CHAPTER VIII

INFLUENCE ON SPECIAL FORMS OF EDUCATION

EDUCATION OF WOMEN

Clinton's most significant relation to the higher education of women is through the academies. But, by way of introduction and because of its own significance, we shall state the provisions made by the Free School Society for the elementary education of girls. In this connection it will be necessary to state some preliminary facts regarding the Female Association.

In March, 1798, there was formed by several ladies of the Quaker persuasion an "Association for the Relief of the Sick Poor." While only Quakers could become members, it was provided that no relief be afforded to any of the people called Quakers. The purpose of the society was wider than the name indicates, for in 1801 they opened a school for boys and girls providing "that instruction which was best suited to the conditions." Their plans are indicated in the following quotation:

"The Association of Women Friends for the Relief of the Poor, having concluded that a part of their funds should be appropriated to the education of poor children of the following description, *viz.,* those whose parents belong to no religious society, and who, from some cause or other, cannot be admitted into any of the charity schools of this city, have appointed the following persons as a committee to open a school for that purpose: Lydia P. Mott, Caroline Bowne, Sarah Collins, May Minturn, Jr., Hannah Bowne, and Susan Collins, who have, agreeably to permission, rented a room at the rate of £16 per annum, and engaged a widow woman of good education and morals as an instructor, and allowed her a salary of £30 a year to be advanced at the discretion of the committee which met at the school room, on the 28th of the 12 month."[1]

---

[1]Bourne, p. 653.

These women became convinced that their plans could be much more advantageously prosecuted by admitting only girls, and they therefore discharged the boys.

It will be readily noticed that the germ of the Free School Society is contained in the efforts of these ladies. The field of endeavor of both would have been the same. The discharge of the boys made some provision for them necessary. We can readily believe that the Female Association interested the men in the proposition, when we remember the character of these women, and especially the fact that several of the leaders of the association were members of the families of the trustees of the Free School Society.

The Free School Society provided in almost all of its schools accommodations for the association's girls. Soon after the Free School No. 1 was erected, accommodations were offered to and accepted by the association, and about six years later an additional room was provided for it. In December, 1811, apartments in No. 2 were offered and accepted as a school for girls. Similar provisions with similar oversight were made in the successive buildings until 1828 when the association ceased to conduct schools for girls. This was due to the fact that the law of 1828 deprived the association of a share of the school fund. With its own funds thereafter the association conducted infant schools.

By the law of 1813 schools not incorporated were excluded from the benefits of the Common School Fund. The friends of the association immediately took action and the association was incorporated by an act of March 26, 1813. Another act passed April 12, 1819, permitted the association to use the school money for purposes other than that for the payment of teachers' salaries. We may be sure that Clinton's influence was at the service of the society in both instances.

As already noted, Clinton in his message of 1819 said, "Beyond initiatory instruction the education of the female sex is utterly excluded from the contemplation of our laws." This was remedied at the session of 1819; for on March 19 there was passed an act to incorporate the Female Academy at Waterford.[2] Com-

---

[2]Chap. 52, Laws of 1819.

menting on this, Clinton said: "As this is the first attempt ever made in this country to promote the education of the female sex by the patronage of the government . . . . I trust that you will not be deterred by *common-place ridicule* from extending your munificence to this meritorious institution."

The next year, another female academy or seminary was incorporated, still another in 1821, two more in 1822 and an act passed for the relief of the trustees of the Albany Female Academy, and one in 1825. These were: in 1820, March 24,[3] the Female Seminary in the village of Catskill; in 1821, Feb. 6,[4] the Female Academy in the City of Albany; in 1822, March 15,[5] the Female Seminary at Newtown, Long Island, and on April 12,[6] the Female Academy in Cooperstown, and in 1825, April 14,[7] the Female Seminary in Canandaigua. During the year of Clinton's death (1828), two female academies were incorporated. The Albany Female Seminary (April 9),[8] and the Cortland Female Seminary (April 18),[9] and an act was passed to relieve the Cooperstown Female Academy (April 19).[10]

The Female Seminary in the village of Catskill was the only institution not organized.[11] All these institutions were in existence at the middle of the century and many are in existence to-day. It may be well to indicate briefly the progress of the movement for the ten succeeding years. During 1829 and 1830 no academies were incorporated; during 1831 one was, the Buffalo Female Seminary,[12] which, however, was not admitted by the Regents. In 1833 the Bernville Academy and Female Seminary[13] was incorporated, but was not organized. In 1834 the Poughkeepsie Female Seminary was incorporated.[14] During the next year no female academy or seminary was incorporated, but during the four succeeding years twelve more were incorporated. In 1836 three, the Fulton Female Seminary,[15] the Mount Pleasant Female Seminary[16] and the Poughkeepsie Female Academy;[17] in 1837

---

[3]Chap. 106, Laws of 1820.
[4]Chap. 53, Laws of 1821.
[5]Chap. 53, Laws of 1822.
[6]Chap. 183, Laws of 1822.
[7]Chap. 149, Laws of 1825.
[8]Chap. 189, Laws of 1828.
[9]Chap. 256, Laws of 1828.
[10]Chap. 282, Laws of 1828.

[11]Hough, p. 597.
[12]Chap. 227, Laws of 1831.
[13]Chap. 51, Laws of 1833.
[14]Chap. 40, Laws of 1834.
[15]Chap. 447, Laws of 1836.
[16]Chap. 288, Laws of 1836.
[17]Chap. 286, Laws of 1836.

four; the Rochester Female Academy,[18] the Schenectady Young Ladies' Institute,[19] the Troy Female Seminary[20] (which had been in existence with Mrs. Willard as principal since 1821), and the Utica Female Academy;[21] in 1838 three, the Auburn Female Seminary,[22] the Batavia Female Academy,[23] and the Rutgers Female Institute;[24] in 1839 two, the Amsterdam Female Seminary[25] and the Seward Female Seminaries.[26]

It is noteworthy at this point that in the seven years after Clinton's death but three female academies were incorporated, and of these three one was not organized, and one was refused admission to the University by the Regents.

Summary. When it is remembered that in 1819 the secondary education of girls was, to use Clinton's phrase, a matter of common-place ridicule, and that in the succeeding nine years eight female academies were incorporated, only one of which was not organized, great credit must be given to Clinton for his championship of so worthy a cause and more for the results that were accomplished. The almost total collapse of the movement after his death is, from the legislative standpoint, indirect evidence of the strength of his influence. However, after 1835 the movement acquired new strength.

EDUCATION OF JUVENILE DELINQUENTS

B. K. Pierce in his book "A Half Century with Juvenile Delinquents," which is a history of the New York House of Refuge, says: "De Witt Clinton was Governor of the State; the managers of the House of Refuge were his intimate friends; he had become personally interested in their benevolent movements and familiar with the discipline of the new institution. The Governor ever remained a strong friend of the House of Refuge. Mr. Maxwell in his happy speech at the opening of the present House in referring to the early friends of the institution spoke warmly of Governor Clinton." This statement, together with the quota-

---

[18]Chap. 231, Laws of 1837.
[19]Chap. 283, Laws of 1837.
[20]Chap. 339, Laws of 1837.
[21]Chap. 284, Laws of 1837.
[22]Chap. 279, Laws of 1838.

[23]Chap. 55, Laws of 1838.
[24]Chap. 192, Laws of 1838.
[25]Chap. 3, Laws of 1839.
[26]Chap. 130, Laws of 1839.

tion from the messages, shows that in this problem Clinton was keenly interested and actively engaged. How successful his advocacy of the needs of the Society for Juvenile Delinquents, is indicated below.

During the interim between Clinton's two periods as Governor (on March 29, 1824) there was passed "An act to incorporate the Society for the Reformation of Juvenile Delinquents in the City of New York." The most significant section of the act follows:

"And be it further enacted that the said managers shall have power in their discretion to receive and take into the House of Refuge, to be established by them all such children who shall be taken up or committed as vagrants or convicted of criminal offenses in the said city, as may, in the judgment of the Court of General Sessions of the peace (or other proper authority) . . . . be proper objects, and the said managers shall have power to place the children committed to their care, during the minority of said children at such employment, and to cause them to be instructed in such branches of useful knowledge as shall be suitable to their years and capacities, and they shall have power in their discretion to bind out the said children with their consent as apprentices, as servants during their minority to such persons and at such places, to learn such proper trades and employments as in their judgment will do most for the reformation and amendment and the future benefit and advantage of such children. Provided such charge and power . . . . shall not extend to females beyond the age of 18 years."

Clinton became Governor in 1825. He made no specific recommendation except to remind the Legislature of their duty, because as he said: "I understand that a board composed of intelligent men have been charged by the Legislature to consider this subject and that their report will in due time be presented to you." However, there was passed, April 9, 1825,[27] "An act in Aid of the Managers of the Society for Juvenile Delinquents in the City of New York." It provided for the payment to the society, out of moneys not otherwise appropriated, the sum of two thousand dollars annually for five years—the first payment to be made on May 1, 1825.

In the 1826 message we have the noteworthy commendation

---

[27]Chap. 107, Laws of 1825.

of the institution as the "best penitentiary institution ever devised by the wit and established by the beneficence of man."

During the same month—January 28, 1826—there was passed "An act to amend an act entitled 'An act to incorporate the Society for the Reformation of Juvenile Delinquents in the City of New York, passed March 29, 1824,' and for other purposes."[28] This act provided that "the managers . . . . shall receive and take into the House of Refuge all such children as shall be convicted of criminal offenses in *any* city or county of this state." The duties of the managers are the same as in the original act. It provided also by way of support that the commissioners in charge of the Marine Hospital should pay over to the Juvenile Delinquent Society all money in excess of the expenses. In addition it provided that they shall "also pay the balance or surplus as the one administering the government may think necessary for the erection of a House of Refuge for Female Juvenile Delinquents." The one "administering the government" apparently thought a House of Refuge for Juvenile Delinquents necessary, for we find in the message of 1827:

"The provision made at the session for the extension and support, in the City of New York, of a House of Refuge for juvenile delinquents has been faithfully and beneficially applied. A separate and accommodating building has been erected for females, and schools on the monitorial plan have been successfully established. The institution now contains 131 males and 30 females who have been rescued from the most abject debasement and it is preventive as well as remedial in its influence. It must be considered a noble, as well as successful experiment in favor of humanity."

Summary. Clinton's interest in the work of the Society for the Reformation of Juvenile Delinquents was shown by his elaborate and enthusiastic comments in his messages. These messages, too, were not without legislative effect. There was no specific reference to the society in the 1825 message, though an appropriation act was passed the following April, which Clinton approved. The extension of the work of the society recommended by the message of 1826 was embodied in Chapter 24, Laws of 1826. This law provided, at the option of the one administering the govern-

---

[28]Chap. 24, Laws of 1826.

ment (Clinton), for a House of Refuge for Female Juvenile Delinquents.   Clinton exercised his option, for in the 1826 message,
is found the statement that adequate provision had been made for
women.

EDUCATION OF DEAF AND DUMB

The beginnings for the education for the deaf and dumb were
not auspicious.   The men interested in the movement were not
getting along amicably.   Clinton in a letter dated from Albany,
Dec. 16, 1817, to a person connected with the Hartford Institution, says: "I received your two letters respecting the education
of the Deaf and Dumb and thank you for these kind attentions.
An institution for that purpose has been incorporated and organized in New York, but it has done nothing.   The first requisite
is to raise funds and when I was lately in that city I turned my attention to the subject, but the truth is there is so much littleness
on the part of many of the managers that I am afraid nothing
efficient will be done."

However, in the message of January, 1819, Clinton could say
that "the New York Institution for the instruction of the Deaf
and Dumb has deserved well of the friends of humanity and that
he cherishes the fullest confidence that you (the Legislature)
will take this interesting establishment under your especial protection and that your munificence will only be exceeded by its
merits."   The act of incorporation made De Witt Clinton president.   In the list of names and addresses of officers and directors
we find naturally the names of many friends of Clinton.   In the
list of those elected May 22, 1819, Clinton's name is found in the
list of directors.

To what extent the Legislature responded to the appeal of
Clinton the following facts show.   It will be necessary at first,
however, to refer back to the article of incorporation.   The act
to incorporate the members of the New York Institution for the
Deaf and Dumb had been passed April 15, 1817.[29]   It was formed
according to this act, "for the purpose of affording the necessary
means of instruction for the Deaf and Dumb—and also provides for the support and maintenance of those in that condition
whose parents are unable to maintain them during their course of

---

[29]Chap. 244, Laws of 1817.

tuition." The act made the members a body corporate and politic in fact and in name, with the usual privileges. It was to continue in force until April 1, 1837, and the act is declared to be a public act.

An act relative to Lotteries was passed April 13, 1819.[30] Section 36 provides that half of the fines and forfeitures under this act shall go to the person who shall prosecute violations of it, and the other half, if offenses are committed in the City of New York, shall be equally divided between this institution and the Free School Society. Section 38 provided that these institutions should report to the Comptroller the several sums received. The same day another act was passed. This was "An act in Aid of the New York Institution for the Instruction of the Deaf and Dumb."[31] This act appropriated for the institution the sum of ten thousand dollars, provided no part of the sum shall be used for purchase of land or erection of building, and required an annual report.

Section 13 of "An act to provide for the payment of certain officers of government and for other purposes" passed April 3, 1821,[32] provides that two thousand five hundred dollars shall be paid to the treasurer for the charitable purposes of the institution during the ensuing year.

There was passed on April 16, 1822, "An act to provide for the instruction of the indigent deaf and dumb within this state."[33] Without going into the machinery of selecting the pupils, this act provided that each senate district (of which there were eight) was entitled to send four indigent deaf and dumb persons between the ages of ten and twenty-five to the institution. These were to be provided with board and tuition for a period not exceeding three years. The state was to pay one hundred and fifty dollars per year for each pupil. It was further provided that if there were any indigent deaf and dumb still remaining, the supervisors of the county could send them on the same terms as the state, adding only their travelling expenses. This money was to be raised and levied according to the sixth section of the act to support common schools.

---

[30]Chap. 212, Laws of 1819.
[31]Chap. 238, Laws of 1819.
[32]Chap. 22, Laws of 1821.
[33]L. B., v. 12, p. 59.

In response to a letter from Clinton dated December 20, 1824, Samuel Akerly, Secretary of the Institution, advises him that the present age limits should be maintained, and at the suggestion of the head teacher adds that the period of instruction should be increased to five or six years. The "Act extending and supplementary to certain acts providing for the Indigent Deaf and Dumb within the State," was passed April 18, 1825, and extended the period of instruction to four years.[34] It extended the act five years from May 1, 1826. It provided, further, that pupils might be taken from districts already sending the full number allowed to them until the limit established by law for the entire state was reached. This act also provided for a second asylum—The Central Asylum.

"An act to provide for the building of an asylum for the deaf and dumb in the City of New York," passed March 23, 1827,[35] appropriated ten thousand dollars upon the condition that the institution raise an equal sum. It also provided:

"That it shall be the duty of the Superintendent of Common Schools from time to time to inquire into the expenses of said institution and the system of instruction pursued therein; to visit and inspect the schools and the lodgings of the pupils; to ascertain by a comparison with other similar institutions, whether any improvement can be made, and for that purpose to appoint such and so many persons as he shall from time to time deem necessary, visitors of the said school; to suggest to the Directors and to the Legislature such improvements as he shall deem expedient and report annually to the Legislature in all the matters aforesaid and particularly the conditions of the schools, the improvement of the pupils and their treatment in respect to their board and their lodging."

On April 15, 1830, an act was passed almost doubling the number of state pupils and extending the act five years from May 1, 1831.

Summary. Clinton was made president of the Society for the first year by the act of incorporation and continued during the following years as a director. He did not retain the presidency because of his election as Governor. His appeals to the Legis-

---

[34]Chap. 189, Laws of 1825.
[35]Chap. 97, Laws of 1827.

lature found immediate response in the acts which have just been passed in review. These provided generously for the financial support of the institutions, especially the New York City one, for an effective means of organization and oversight. for increasing facilities for the instruction of deaf and dumb, for increasing the numbers who may profit by such instruction, and for lengthening the term during which the deaf and dumb may be instructed.

AGRICULTURAL EDUCATION

There was given in Chapter III Clinton's complete program as outlined in his message of 1818. The recommendations contained therein were not carried into effect during the session of 1818. As a result we find the following statement in the message of 1819: "I have to express my regret at the failure of a measure generally admitted to be proper and expedient, on account of a difference of opinion as to its modifications. That this important pursuit is the foundation of wealth, power and prosperity; that it requires the energies of the mind, as well as the labor of the body; that it demands the light of science to guide its progress, and munificence of government to accelerate its movement, to extend its usefulness and to diffuse its blessings, are positions which can not be controverted." After much further pointed discussion he recommends: "The Board of Agriculture ought also to be invested with authority to make a statistical survey of the State and to obtain periodical return of births, marriages and deaths . . . . complete information of the state of the country, with a view to its melioration, would effect great improvements in the practical pursuits of life, would open new and important views in the science of political philosophy; a science of all others the most interesting and the least understood. The special designation of a fund for these objects either by some of the expedients proposed at the session, or by others which can be easily devised, is required by every description of public spirit and public duty."

The effect of this was the act of April 7, 1819.[36] The first section of this act provided an appropriation of ten thousand dollars annually for two years for the promotion of agriculture and family domestic manufacturers. It further apportioned the amount

---

[36]Chap. 107, Laws of 1819.

among the various counties, e.g., Albany was to receive three hundred and fifty dollars.

Section two provided that any agricultural society which would secure by voluntary subscription any sum of money and subscribe an affidavit to be filed with the comptroller should receive an equal amount, "not, however, in any case exceeding the amount to which such county or counties would be entitled according to the apportionment aforesaid."

In the message of 1820 there is a statement of Clinton's evident pleasure at the passage of the bill during the last session. But not satisfied he observes that the excellence of the provisions for the promotion of agriculture may be "augmented" by extending the duration of the act, by augmenting the fund and by enlarging the powers of the supervisory board. This resulted in the passage of the act of March 24, 1820,[37] entitled "An act to extend an act entitled 'An act to improve the agriculture of this state,' passed April 7, 1819, and for other purposes." Section one extended the provisions of the act for four years with the exception of the eighth and last clause. Section two provided an appropriation of five hundred dollars "to enable them (the members of the Board of Agriculture) to buy such books as they deem necessary to aid them in publishing their annual volume and in the diffusion of correct agricultural information." It provided further for an annual appropriation of one hundred seventy five dollars for five years for the counties of Cattaraugus and Niagara, provided they should form an agricultural society. The fourth section authorized that the Legislature might at any time amend or repeal the act.

TECHNICAL EDUCATION

Clinton's most significant relation to the education of mechanics, apart from his encouragement of apprentices' libraries, is in connection with the Rensselaer School. A word may be said about two other institutions: The General Society of Mechanics and Tradesmen of the City of New York, and the Mechanic and Scientific Institute. Clinton approved on January 26, 1821, "An act to amend an act entitled 'An act relative to the General Society of Mechanics and Tradesmen in the City of New York,

---

[37]Chap. 97, Laws of 1820.

passed April 3, 1811,' " which permitted the society to "appropriate part of their funds to the support of a school for the gratuitous education of the children of deceased or indigent members of the said society, and also to the establishment of an apprentice library, for the use of the apprentices of mechanics in the City of New York." Section two provided that the society "may be by law entitled to a portion of the money, arising from the general school fund."

Clinton approved the next year (March 22, 1822) the act incorporating the Mechanic and Scientific Institute. The preamble informs us that the association was formed for the "purpose of instituting and maintaining scientific and practical lectures applicable to the acts, and for collecting and forming a repository of machinery, tools, and generally, for enlarging the knowledge and improving the condition of mechanics, artisans and manufacturers." In the message of 1825 is a recommendation in favor of the institution, "the first organized school of its kind in the world." Therein Clinton recommended that the City and State may grant from contiguous property, owned by them and unoccupied, an appropriate site on which the institution may construct a building adequate for its purposes. The site was granted.

The incorporation of the Rensselaer School must have pleased Clinton immensely. Here was a splendid illustration of what Clinton had already said of the Mechanic and Scientific Institute of New York that "it is destined to increase the character of our mechanic interest, by applying philosophy to the arts, and imparting the benefits of science to that most useful body of our fellow citizens." It was the practical embodiment of what Clinton praised so highly in his Phi Beta Kappa address: the experimental method of Bacon. It was, too, a big step in restoring the "most important interest and the most numerous calling—agriculture—to its merited intellectual rank." And again it was in line with Clinton's recommendation in his message of the very year of the incorporation of the school. After stating that agriculture "demands and deserves your fostering patronage," he goes on to say: "A wide and unexplored field lies before us. Experimental and pattern farms, plantation of useful trees for ship building, architecture and fuel; labor saving machines; improved seeds and plants of those productions now used; new modes of cultivation, and the whole range of rural economy are subjects deserving your animating support."

On March 21 of the year this recommendation was made Clinton signed the bill which incorporated the Rensselaer School. Because this school deserves greater attention than it has yet received in the history of American education, and because the statement is so similar to what Clinton had been wont to say whenever this subject was discussed, it is well to quote the preamble of this act:

"Whereas the Honorable Stephen Van Rensselaer has procured suitable buildings in the City of Troy in Rensselaer County and there has set up a school and at his own private expense, has furnished the same with a scientific library, chemical and philosophical apparatus, instruments for teaching land surveying, and other branches of practical mathematics which are useful to the agriculturalist, the machinist, and to other artists, and furnished separate and commodious rooms for instruction in natural philosophy, natural history, the common operation of chemicals, and an assay room for the analysis of soils, manures, minerals and animal and vegetable matter with the application of these departments of science to agriculture, domestic economy and the arts.

"And whereas said Van Rensselaer has employed teachers and caused an experimental system of instruction to be adopted by them, whereby each student is required to observe the operation of the select number of agriculturalists and artists in vicinity of said school and to demonstrate the principles upon which the results of such operations depend, by experiment and specimens performed and exhibited by his own hands under the directions of said teachers, and whereas one important object of said school is to qualify teachers for instructing youth in villages and common school districts belonging to the class of foreigners and mechanics, by lectures or otherwise in the application of the most important principles of experimental chemistry, natural philosophy and practical mathematics to agriculture, domestic economy, and art, and manufacturers. And whereas the trustees of said school who were appointed to take charge thereof by said Van Rensselaer by an instrument of writing dated November 5th in the year 1824, had represented to the Legislature that after having tested the plan of said school by a trial of one year, they find it to be practicable and in their opinion highly beneficial to the public. And whereas the Legislature considers it their duty to encourage such laudable efforts and such munificient application of the surplus wealth of individuals," it incorporated the school.

It would seem fair to infer that Clinton had a hand in the plan and organization of this school, because it was the embodiment of so many of his cherished ideas, and because of his personal friendship with the founder, and his service with him on the Board of Canal Commissioners; yet there is no more positive evidence to support the inference.

However, Clinton addressed the Honorable the Assembly on February 8, 1828 as follows: "I lay before you certain proceedings of the trustees of the Rensselaer School at Troy, by which it appears that they offer gratuitous use of the school to the State for the purpose of educating teachers in the application of the experimental sciences to agriculture and the useful arts. The importance of the subject and the liberality of the offer will, I am pursuaded, ensure your attention to this communication." Clinton transmitted with this message (1) the proceedings of the trustees, (2) two letters from Van Rensselaer to Dr. Blatchford. The one dated Albany, November 4, 1826, practically gave Dr. Blatchford complete control of the institution; the other is given below in full, and (3) the letter of transmittal addressed to Governor Clinton dated February 4, 1828. The second letter to Dr. Blatchford follows:

"HOUSE OF REPRESENTATIVES, December 31, 1827.
"DEAR SIR:

"I take the liberty of suggesting to you and the trustees the propriety of offering the school (over which you preside with so much dignity and usefulness) to the Legislature to educate teachers as proposed by Governor Clinton in his message at a former session of the Legislature—perhaps an amendment to the charter extending the power of the trustees to change the location of the school if they deem it necessary."

The Governor's message and the accompanying material were first referred to the Committee on Colleges, Academies and Common Schools, and then to the Regents. The Regents returned a highly favorable report signed by John Tayler, Chancellor, and Gideon Hawley, Secretary. One paragraph may be here quoted:

"The public advantages to be derived from accepting the offer of the trustees of the Rensselaer School derive their principal importance from the consideration, 1st, That a knowledge of the science taught in that school is indispensable to the improvement and permanence of our manufacturing establishment, 2d, That this knowledge may be obtained there in a shorter time, at less expense and in a more efficient form than in any other existing school, and 3d, That the public interest requires its diffusion in the most expeditious way and most practical form."[38]

The matter was again referred to the Committee on Colleges, Academies and Common Schools. But apparently nothing became of it. Probably if Clinton had lived, his power and influence would have secured favorable action in the matter.

Summary. Clinton had deep and abiding interest in the education of mechanics. Apparently his election to the governorship was a signal for attempts to secure legislative enactments, for we have the act amending the charter of the General Society of Mechanics and Tradesmen of New York City and the act incorporating the Mechanic and Scientific Institute passed by the Legislature and signed by Clinton during his first period of governorship. His most significant relation to the education of mechanics is through the Rensselaer School. This was incorporated at the beginning of Clinton's second period of governorship. It was the expression of so many of Clinton's cherished ideas that it does not seem unlikely that he was consulted in the organization of the institution. The transmission of the special message of 1827 to the Legislature, together with the accompanying material, showed that at that time Clinton was in consultation with the officers of the school. The change proposed by the founder had its inspiration in a previous message of Clinton's. Clinton died a week after the special message was transmitted. We can be sure that had he lived the proposition would have been accepted by the State.

MEDICAL EDUCATION

Clinton was especially interested in medical education. As a Regent of the University his work was devoted mainly to the medical schools. His relations with medical education center about his work as a Regent and his recommendations as Governor.[39] His work as Regent settled the disgraceful quarrels be-

---

[38]New York State *Assembly Journal*, 1829, p. 282.

[39]Clinton's work as a Regent was largely concerned with the College of Physicians and Surgeons. He was one of a committee of three to report on

tween the rival medical faculties and gave New York at least one efficient medical school. His recommendations as Governor related to raising the educational requirements and protecting the New York schools from the rivalry of institutions in neighboring states having inferior educational requirements.

The first topic relates to Clinton's connection with the medical colleges. A full medical faculty was organized in connection with Columbia in 1769, and in May, 1770, the first degree of M. D. was granted in America. But the institution did not prosper and was discontinued. In the autumn of 1791 the private association, under the superintendence of Nicholas Romayne introduced no fewer than sixty medical students into the college and thereby prevailed on the Legislature of the state to make a grant of $30,000 to the trustees for the purpose of enabling them to enlarge their building. But owing to "internal jealousies and outward prejudices," the institution did not prosper and was finally discontinued in 1810.

However, in the meantime, the Regents of the University, being satisfied that a proposed institution in the City of New York might be "of public importance in the diffusing the knowledge of the healing art," granted to the Medical Society of the County of New York a charter incorporating the members of the Society into a College of Physic and Surgery with all the rights and privileges as might conduce to the promotion of medical knowledge and public good. Here, too, the "internal jealousies and outward prejudices" were at work. In April, 1811, a committee of the Regents reported "that unfortunate misunderstandings have taken place between several professors of that institution, which have already materially impeded its operation and unless something effectual be done by the Regents, it will become degraded in the estimation of the public and its usefulness be inevitably destroyed." The report goes on to

---

the "professorships and officials proper to be established for the College of Physicians and Surgeons," and such regulations as will be necessary to carry into effect the charter (Minutes of the Regents, Ms., v. 1, p. 289). We notice Clinton's share in the union of the College of Physicians and Surgeons and the Medical School of Columbia College. The report of the College of Physicians and Surgeons was frequently referred to Clinton. On page 322 of volume 1, and page 127 of volume 2 of the Minutes of the Regents we find able and elaborate reports made by Clinton on this subject.

state that the union of both medical colleges was an object of the first importance.[40]

The suggestion apparently originated with Clinton. At least Dr. Hosack said: "At that time the Mayor of this city, a member of the Board of Regents (De Witt Clinton), communicated to me an outline of the measures which in his opinion would be proper to adopt in order to place the medical school upon a permanent basis.

"The great object proposed was to unite, as far as was possible, the talents of both medical schools.

"Having thus freely expressed my individual opinion upon the arrangements proposed, I also at the suggestion of Mr. Clinton called a meeting of the Faculty of Physic of Columbia College and communicated to them the contemplated plan of union."[41]

At a meeting of the Regents, April 1, 1811, it was "Resolved: That the Regents living in the City of New York be a committee to visit, in the recess, Columbia College and the College of Physicians and Surgeons and the Academy in the southern district, and that they be authorized to signify to the Trustees of Columbia College that the object of the Regents in uniting the medical institutions of said city is by combining the talents of the professors in one seminary to render the state of medical education more respectable and useful and that the said committee be further authorized to request, in behalf of the Regents, the cooperation of the said trustees, in carrying out the new arrangements into effect."[42]

Clinton and the other Regents living in New York City submitted the following report:

To the Regents of the University of the State of New York:

The Regents of the University having authorized the members of that Board residing in the City of New York to effect a union between the College of Physicians and Surgeons and Faculty of Physic attached to Columbia College, the underwritten have the honor to report that this object, so important to medical science,

---

[40]Hough, p. 380. The references to Hough are given rather than directly to the manuscript Minutes of the Regents because the former is the more accessible.

[41]Hosack's Observations, p. 2.

[42]Minutes, Board of Regents, v. 2, p. 24.

has been accomplished with their approbation and satisfactorily to all concerned.

The increased number of students and the flourishing condition of the College already exhibit the benefits which such an auspicious arrangement was calculated to produce. It was necessary to extend the list of professors in order to effect this coalition and as this has, of course, produced a correspondent combination of information and talents, the underwritten earnestly recommend it to the Regents to sanction the arrangement without any alteration. To omit any of the professors that have been nominated would have an invidious appearance and might reintroduce that spirit of discord which is now happily extinguished.

And the underwritten would further respectfully suggest to the board the expediency of not making any new appointments or arrangements in relation to this establishment unless rendered absolutely necessary. The College is now in a flourishing way. and the Regents having done all that duty and the interests of the institution requires, any further interposition might have a tendency to check instead of accelerating its prosperity.

Dated 22d of January. 1814.

DE WITT CLINTON,
MATTHEW CLARKSON,
HENRY RUTGERS.[43]

Clinton's efficient aid in securing support for the College of Physicians and Surgeons is indicated in the following paragraph from the "Memoir of De Witt Clinton." (1828)[44]

"The honor of the munificent appropriations made to our various seminaries of learning must be shared by him with others, but it would be unjust in me, a member of the medical profession, not to acknowledge the debt of obligations in behalf of the College of Physicians and Surgeons by which an institution humble and unpretending in its commencement, has been enabled in a few years, to have held honorable competition with the oldest and most powerful medical school in our country."

The second topic relates to Clinton's influence on medical education during the period that he was Governor. References are found to medicine and surgery in the messages of 1818, 1819, 1820, and 1826. The first is probably the most significant. It is quoted in full in the preceding chapter and may be here summarized. After commenting on the fact that an educated physi-

---

[43]Hough, pp. 156-7.
[44]P. 46.

cian is not only a conservator of health, but a missionary of science, he goes on to urge "a law rendering attendance upon lectures in the university an indispensable passport to medical practise." The immediate effect of this—though all that was urged was not secured—was Chapter 206 of the Laws of 1818, passed April 20. It provided besides the details of appeal from the decision of county societies, a number of censors, etc., that after May 1, 1821, a person to be admitted to examination as a candidate to practice physic and surgery in New York State, must have studied medical science for four years after his sixteenth year of age with a regular physician and surgeon. It provided, further, (1) that the requirement for any portion of this time not exceeding a year could be satisfied by attendance in either medical college of the state and (2) that persons attending one or more complete courses of lectures delivered by each of the professors in all branches of medical science in the medical institutions of this state or elsewhere, could count such attendance in lieu of one year of study.

A further step in advance was taken the next year in Chapter 247 of the Laws of 1819, passed April 13. The second section of this act provided that no student should be granted the degree of doctor of medicine until he fully completed the requirements as noted above and "shall also in addition thereto have attended a complete course of lectures delivered by each of the professors of such college."

The next measure, apart from those bearing on the support of the medical colleges and those in relation to the county societies, was preventive. It was "An act relative to the degree of doctor of medicine conferred by colleges without the state." This law may be quoted in full. It was enacted,

"That all diplomas granted by authorities out of this state to individuals who have pursued their studies in any medical college not recognized by the laws of this state shall be void and have no effect as it regards authorizing the said individuals to practice physic and surgery in this state."[45]

Summary. At the end of the first decade of the nineteenth century there were in New York City two medical schools, the

---

[45]Chap. 185, Laws of 1827.

one attached to Columbia College, and the College of Physicians and Surgeons. Neither was eminently successful because its work was hampered both internally and externally. To Clinton it seemed desirable to unite the two institutions and, thereby, secure to New York at least one successful medical school. Clinton was made chairman of the committee of the Board of Regents to effect this union, which, according to the report of January 22, 1814, was accomplished to the satisfaction of all concerned. As Governor he continued his interest in the institution and so recommended it frequently and successfully to the patronage of the Legislature. Two other valuable things recommended by Clinton were brought to pass by the Legislature with his own approval as Governor, namely, making attendance at a university a necessary, though, at first, it is merely a permissive qualification to become a doctor of medicine, and preventing doctors with inferior qualification from outside of New York from practising within the State.

CHAPTER IX

THE SIGNIFICANCE OF CLINTON'S EDUCATIONAL INFLUENCE

THE PROBLEM OF THE CHAPTER

The first two chapters furnished the background for the present study—a statement of the physical, social and educational conditions at the beginning of the nineteenth century. The third chapter stated the educational views of Clinton largely in his own words for reasons heretofore explained. In Chapters V, VI, VII, and VIII, was stated the educational influence of Clinton, both the direct and indirect. These four chapters were statements of the facts. There was no attempt to state the significance of these facts. Their significance when viewed in the light of subsequent history lies in this truth: that Clinton is entitled to a secure place— and by no means a minor one—in the history of American education. The detailed statement of this is the problem of this chapter.

To Clinton belongs all the prestige of the pioneer. However, his place is due not merely to the fact that he was among the first in the field, but to the worth of the results accomplished. And when it is remembered that these were the results of pioneer efforts we will the more readily grant, I think, the contention that Clinton is one of our great American educators.

THE CHANGED CONDITIONS IN 1830

There can be no doubt in the mind of the student of the history of New York State during this period that there was an intellectual and moral awakening.[1] It may be called, too, a period of origins

---

[1]By way of confirmation of our own conclusions and because of its pertinence here, we quote the following from Keep's New York Society Library, pp. 316-18:

and organization. The main concern here is the educational aspect. It were a comparatively easy task to show Clinton's share in the moral and humanitarian aspects of the movements from his letter books, from letters written to him, and from his legislative record. It would be found to be as important and extensive as in the intellectual aspect. In fact, the whole educational movement began as a philanthropic-humanitarian movement, and being one expression of it, cannot, possibly, be separated from the other. However, there is excluded from this study Clinton's connection with such institutions as the Sailors Snug Harbor, for instance.

The foregoing statement is proved by contrasting the conditions at the beginning of the century and at the end of our period. In Chapter II there was noted, in a general way, the educational conditions before Clinton took an active part in their improvement. What, then, was accomplished by Clinton and his fellow workers after their efforts of a quarter of a century? The following is a summary statement:

Elementary Education. Probably the greatest achievement was the initiation and development of public elementary schools. In New York City there had been successfully established a system

---

"Within a few years, however, there came a change. Wounds inflicted by the War of 1812 fast turned to unheeded scars; New York was soon again on its bounding course toward predestined supremacy in population and wealth. These strides in local prosperity seem happily to have been attended or closely followed by a deepening inclination to reflect soberly on involved responsibilities. Men felt constrained to look more scathingly to themselves, their manners and their minds (as well as to their creature wants) and to their fellows no less. The period from 1814 to 1830 may fairly be characterized as an age of foundations. Under the influence of a steadily growing humanizing spirit, there began to flourish asylums for the bodily and mentally infirm, institutions to encourage thrift and saving among working people, societies for the relief of the poor and the destitute and a determined effort to ameliorate the moral and physical condition of public offenders.

"Furthermore this moral awakening was accompanied, if not caused by an intellectual stir, and renascence. The growth of American democracy, the discussion of Socialistic views, a reaction against the hitherto accepted tenets of theology, these played a part in stimulating desire for knowledge and its dissemination. Promptings of this nature accordingly led to the formation of such associations as the Literary and Philosophical Society, the Lyceum of Natural History, the New York Law Institute, the American Bible Society and various Episcopal Theological Societies that culminated in the establishment of the General Seminary; the Mercantile and Apprentice Library and other institutions of similar purport. But of them all, the one which seems to have attracted most widespread attention, and which cerof public schools by a semi-public body—the Public School Society. In this society Clinton was easily the dominant personality and without his tremendous political and social influence, the society could not have done its great work.   It was but a step to pass from the control of this system by this society to its control by a board of education, and that step was prepared for in the legislation of 1826 and actually consummated in 1853.   Many of the other private philanthropic societies, aided by Clinton, provided free public education for special groups of normal children, for example: The Economical School Society and the Orphan Asylum Society.   The education of girls was seriously considered at this time and similar means for the elementary and secondary education of boys and girls were provided.   Nor was the education of special classes neglected.   Provision was made for the education of the deaf and dumb in two well-equipped and state-aided institutions.   And a philanthropic society, in which Clinton was interested, provided educational and other facilities for the reformation of juvenile delinquents.

The movement for free public schools was by no means confined to New York City.   The spread of the Lancasterian movement throughout the State and country is evidence of this.   Lan-

---

tainly gathered unto itself the support of the community to a remarkable degree was the New York Atheneum."

The following two letters will be interesting in this connection.   They are another illustration of the fact that when Clinton was not active in an educational or philanthropic movement he was probably consulted:

"ALBANY, 9 August, 1824.

"GENTLEMEN :

"I feel honored by your invitation to pronounce an address at the opening of the Atheneum and highly appreciate the principles and the organization of the institution.   I should be happy to show my respect for them and the gentlemen who have favored me with this call, did not my engagements render my attendance impracticable."

(Letter Books, V. 6, p. 212.)

"ALBANY, 9 August, 1824.

"DEAR SIR :

"I am much indebted to you for the pamphlet relative to the New York Atheneum and entirely approve of the constitution and organization of the institution.   It will reflect honor on the City, as well as on its patrons, and do much good to the cause of useful knowledge.

"If you can excite a spirit sufficiently munificient in the community and if the lecturers will devote themselves to the duties assigned to them, I am persuaded that the patriotic and enlightened views of the founders of the institution will be realized."

(Letter Books, V. 6, p. 214.)

casterian societies were incorporated in seven cities of the State and Lancasterian schools were established in many more. In 1828 there were according to the annual report of the State Superintendent 441,856 children under instruction, whereas in 1800 there was no State Superintendent, and all schools were private or charitable and the number attending unknown.

Infant Schools. Steps were taken toward the end of the period, to provide for the education of children below the common school age, from two to six years old, by the Infant School Society, which was organized at Clinton's suggestion. This society received executive sanction in the message of 1827. The movement was continued by the Public School Society and the Female Association.

Higher Education. Higher education likewise made great strides. In 1800 there were 19 academies; in 1830 there were 58. In the 58 academies in 1830 there were 4,303 scholars of whom 2,222 were academic scholars. In 1800 there were 2 colleges: Columbia and the recently organized Union. In 1830 there were 4, the new ones were Hamilton and Geneva. The University of the City of New York was organized in 1831.

Professional Education. Columbia's was the only medical school in the State at the beginning of the century and had but 21 students. In 1807 the College of Physicians and Surgeons was chartered and was combined with Columbia in 1813. In 1831 there were 182 students and 33 graduates in the combined institution. In 1812 the College of Physicians and Surgeons of the Western District was chartered. In 1831 there were 205 students attending and 39 graduates for that year. No law schools existed in the State during this period. At the beginning of the century there were no theological seminaries. In 1830 there were three: The Hamilton Literary and Theological Institute established by the Baptist Education Society incorporated in 1818, the Presbyterian Theological Seminary (1820) and the General Theological Seminary of the Protestant Episcopal Church (1822). It will be noticed that all three were organized during Clinton's first period as Governor.

The Less Formal Educational Agencies. The educational environment was even further extended through state encouragement and aid of the less formal educational agencies: libraries; lyceums of natural history; literary, philosophical, historical, agricultural and scientific societies. In this movement, Clinton was undoubtedly the foremost figure. Positive evidence has been presented to sustain this contention. Indirect evidence vouched for by a contemporary, himself a factor in this movement, is now offered. Professor Renwick says with reference to the Literary and Philosophical Society that "other more important pursuits withdrew him from its meetings, and with his personal attention the prosperity of the society seems to have departed." Again, with reference to the Historical Society and the American Academy of Arts, the same writer says: "The result of his resignation was disaster to both institutions," for, the statement goes on in substance, the distinguished man who succeeded him could not maintain the decided superiority over his fellows which Clinton was always able to maintain.

There was noted at great length in Chapter III Clinton's reiterated and emphatic recommendations of educational institution to legislative patronage. In Chapters VI, VII, and VIII, there was noted the success of these recommendations in the form of grants to special institutions. More significant provision was made for the support of education in the form of school funds. In 1800 the Literature Fund was practically non-existent; in 1830 the principal of the fund was $153,218 and the amount apportioned $10,000, making an average of $172, to each of the academies. The Common School Fund was non-existent in 1800; in 1828, the capital of the fund was $1,630,825.05. The aggregate amount of public money received and expended by the several districts in the payment of wages of duly qualified teachers was $222,995.77, of which $100,000 was paid from the state treasury, $110,542.32, raised by tax upon the several towns and $12,453.45 from the proceeds of gospel and school lots and other local funds.

THE SIGNIFICANCE OF THE LESS FORMAL EDUCATIONAL AGENCIES

In Chapter III, the significance of Clinton's educational views was stated. Not only did Clinton hold such views, but he tried to make them socially effective by impressing them upon those who were administering the social estate and their advisors. He wished to make these views a social leaven. Consequently Clinton expressed them upon every opportune occasion: in his reports as chairman of legislative committees, in his gubernatorial messages to the Legislature, in his addresses and in his correspondence.

The next topic is closely akin to the last. It is the significance of Clinton's influence on the less formal educational agencies. At the beginning of the century there were very few such agencies, but at the end of the first quarter of the century they were considerable in number and various in purpose. Chapter VI contains a statement of Clinton's direct influence in stimulating and organizing some of the typical ones. It is fairly certain that his indirect influence was hardly less potent. In New York at that time those agencies were much more significant as educational forces than now—to a much greater extent they were the centers of intellectual life. They made a much wider appeal. One of the causes of the difference, is the different conceptions of scholarship and learning. The scholarly man, then, was not the specialist in a particular field of knowledge, or in a narrow portion of it, but the general scholar.

But, morever, these agencies offered a means of development and dissemination of the matter in new fields of knowledge and to fairly well organized fields of knowledge which had not been admitted as yet to the curriculum of the educational institutions. This was notoriously true of science and modern history which had not been admitted to the conventional curriculum of Latin, Greek, and mathematics. With the recognition of these fields of knowledge by the academies and colleges, the agencies devoted to them became less significant. They tended to become mere storehouses of documents or museums.

However, Clinton saw their value in the situation in New York at the time, and made them, by his active participation in their work, very much more significant than they would otherwise have become. This is shown by the fact that immediately upon his withdrawal from the active participation in the affairs of these societies, they languished   Nevertheless their usefulness as educational factors persisted long beyond Clinton's time.

The Movement Towards Free Public Schools

Our interest normally centers in the next topic: The statement of Clinton's share in the development of free public schools. That underlying all his efforts and the efforts of his colleagues this was the great idea they were trying to work out, is evident in the report of the Public School Society of the year of Clinton's death. It reads: "The trustees have long been impressed with the conviction that a system of Public Free Schools supported by a general tax, and to which the children of all classes should be admitted as a matter of right, and not of charity, is the most republican plan, best agreeing with the genius of our institutions and best calculated to foster those feelings of independence in the poorer classes of society on which the welfare of the community so much depends."

In the message of 1826 Clinton himself commenting on the important change which has taken place in the free schools of New York says that by an agreement between the corporation of that city and the trustees of the Free School Society their schools are to become public schools and consequently to admit the children of the rich, as well as the poor. "And," the statement continues, "by *this annihilation of factitious distinctions* there will be a strong incentive for the display of talents and a felicitous accommodation to the genius of republican government." The meeting during this year which settled the change of policy of the society—making it a public school society—was attended by Clinton and it was the only one he had attended in eight years. However, though not present at the meetings, his influence in other matters was exerted indirectly, but always powerfully.

An even more forceful expression of Clinton's view is contained in the 1827 message. After saying that seminaries for general education are either not provided in the old world or but imperfectly supplied by Charity and Sunday Schools, he urges upon the Legislature to "spare no exertion *and to shrink from no expense in the promotion of a cause consecrated by religion and enjoined by patriotism*—the cause, let it be repeated, is seminaries for general education," i.e., free public schools.

There can be no doubt, after the foregoing statements have been read, of the end Clinton had in mind. The steps in the evolution toward this goal extend beyond Clinton's time. The steps will now be indicated. As already noted the liberal support of the society secured largely through Clinton's efforts made the steps possible. The society was organized (1805) and incorporated for the establishment of a free school for those poor children who were not being provided for in the religious charity schools. The next step was taken by the act of April 1, 1808, "An act in relation to the Free School Society of New York," which extended the field of the society to all children who are the proper object of a gratuitous education and changed the long and cumbrous name of the society to "The Free School Society."

The next step during Clinton's life—and final one—was provided for in the act of January 28, 1826. This was also "An act in relation to the Free School Society of New York." It changed the name of the society to the "Public School Society" and further extended its powers so as to embrace all children whether the objects of a gratuitous education or not. It permitted the trustees to charge a fee, and still participate in the Common School Fund. The factitious distinctions were not gotten rid of, for a pay system was introduced. Even though the cost was trivial, varying from twenty-five cents to two dollars, it worked very unsatisfactorily.

It will be well to follow briefly the results of this act of 1826. In February, 1827, a committee was appointed to report the effects for the pay system. They reported that the true and legitimate system for the public schools would be to open their doors to all classes of children free of any expense and the only branches that should be taught are such as have been designated, *viz.*, reading, spelling, writing and arithmetic. However, the committee recommended that the fees be continued and that the maximum fee be one dollar per quarter, and that the higher branches be taught only to the more meritorious and by way of reward. This report was not acted upon. However, a similar report was accepted later.

On February 2, 1832, it was resolved: "That the pay system be abolished." During this same year the carrying out of the permissive provisions of the act of 1826 providing for the conveying of the society's property to the city and receiving it back in perpetual lease was proposed and discussed but was not acted upon. It was finally acted upon before the dissolution of the society in 1853 when the Board of Education assumed control of the school property, etc., and naturally assumed all the privileges of the Free School Society.

In short, the act of January, 1826, practically prepared the way for free schools in New York City. It was an impossibility at that time for any one to accomplish so much for the State as a whole.

THE MOVEMENT FOR THE PROFESSIONAL TRAINING OF TEACHERS

It is a truism that as the teacher so the school. Clinton knew this; knew that a scheme of education might be perfect as machinery, and yet fail miserably if it were not controlled, guided, and utilized by effective and informed personalities. The teacher is the school. This statement leads to another of Clinton's contributions: the adequate conception of the need for the professional training of teachers and a partial satisfaction of it in practise. It has been noticed already that with the trustees of the Free School Society (of which Clinton was one) as early as 1814 it was "an object of great interest to train up young men for the office of instructor in similar schools," and that the realization of such an object was in part accomplished. This appears to be the first actual provision in the United States for specially training teachers for their work. In 1819 the society included in its annual report an invitation to those who might wish to secure a competent knowledge of the Lancasterian movement, to do so, free of expense, in the schools of the society.

Clinton's recommendation in 1826 of a seminary for the education of teachers was not carried into effect until 1844—the Albany Normal School. The immediate result of Clinton's work was the organization of teachers' departments in the academies. This was provided for in the act of 1827, but only indirectly. It received direct legislative sanction in 1835. This was probably the best means for professional preparation at that time—at least it was the only means that could be utilized. It was unquestionably a means of educating the people and the Legislature to the fact that professional training should include more than a knowledge of the subject matter and some lectures on "principles of teaching." It taught them, further, that what was wanted were not schools where professional training was an incidental, but the prime object of the institution. Here as elsewhere "Governor Clinton was far in advance of even the educated public opinion of the State."[2]

THE LANCASTERIAN SYSTEM

Clinton was not primarily interested in method, though, in carrying out his ideas, it was quite essential that he consider the means, i.e., the question of method. He was convinced that the Lancasterian method of mutual instruction was the best possible. The things that especially appealed to him are indicated in the address of 1809:

"It (the Lancasterian system) comprehends reading, writing, arithmetic and the knowledge of Holy Scriptures. It arrives at its object with the least possible trouble and expense. Its distinguished characters are economy, facility and expedition, and its peculiar improvements are cheapness, activity, order and emulation. . . . . Instruction is carried on through the instrumentality of the scholars. The discipline of the school is enforced by shame rather than by infliction of pain."

One other significant characteristic not mentioned above, but contained in the message of 1818, is that the Lancasterian system operated with the same efficacy in education that labor-saving machinery does in the useful arts. Clinton came later to believe that the system was adapted to the higher grade of instruction and hence in 1828 we have his county monitorial high school recommendation.

To Clinton the system was superlatively good, and he held fast to that which he believed good. Clinton's faith in the system was firm and could not be shaken. It is easy for us to see the weaknesses of the system—its mechanical and formal character; the impossibility of having monitors take the place of trained teachers; its fundamental misconception, that teaching is merely the imparting of information, and not a human experience in which a relatively immature and undeveloped personality meets a more developed one and is enriched

There were those in Clinton's day who saw the weaknesses. A man named Hutton sent to Clinton on January 13, 1818, an elaborate critique of the method. After stating that the Lancasterian system has been his peculiar study for the past five years and for part of that period the business of his life he says: "the experience of a few years, I am persuaded, will reduce that system to its original and proper sphere—the instruction of those who cannot otherwise obtain instruction." "There is economy," he observes, "because one teacher is paid where ten are actually employed." He further points out that the monitors are ignorant, that the education of the bright boy selected as monitor practically stops, that the physician has gotten credit for what is nature's due. But probably the most significant sentence, at least the most interesting, follows: "But I presume you never saw that system in operation but when De Witt Clinton was present. When such a name was whispered round the school, what stillness! what subordination! what assiduity!"

However, one gets nowhere by pointing out the weaknesses of the system. The important question is: "What is its significance?" The following is an answer to that question.

From the narrow standpoint of teaching its great contribution was a technique of classroom management and instruction. It was a step in the direction of class instruction, rather than individual instruction. Lancasterian schools were graded schools and graded in each subject. The discipline was mild, and was enforced through shame rather than by the infliction of pain.

But from a larger standpoint, and this is its great significance and our chief concern, it was a long step in the way of free public education. It accustomed people to send their children to schools and to contribute to the support of these schools; it led first to state aid and finally to state support. The lure in the system was its cheapness. At the beginning of the century it would have been impossible to secure state support for any expensive educational system. As already remarked the Lancasterian system attracted people and was supported. The people thereby became accustomed to support their schools. Apparently, once launched upon the policy they continued to do so as a matter of habit, even though education became more expensive, and they did this the more readily when they saw that the free public school was really an implication of their theory of government. The Lancasterian system, however, made the acceptance of the implication a matter of little difficulty.

A Broader Elementary School Curriculum

If Herbert Spencer's question had been proposed to Clinton he would have given Herbert Spencer's answer. The knowledge of most worth is science. However, there would have been differences of detail. In short, the content of education was to be scientific. The statement in the message of 1826 is significant. In this connection, Clinton says: that ten years of the life of a child may be spent in a common school, that in two years the elements of instruction may be acquired and the remaining eight years must either be spent in repetition or in idleness, that with competent teachers of common schools "the outlines of geography, algebra, mineralogy, agriculture, chemistry, mechanical philosophy, surveying, geometry, astronomy, political economy, and ethics might be communicated in that period of time by able preceptors, without essential interference with the calls of domestic industry." When it is remembered that the curriculum of the time consisted of the four R's: reading, 'riting, 'rithmetic and religion (catechism) it can be seen how revolutionary such a proposal was. Here was a serious proposition for the enrichment of the curriculum in the direction of a more scientific content. So far as the elementary schools are concerned this enrichment has had to wait until recent times. As usual Clinton was far in advance of his time educationally.

Scientific Basis for Professional and Technical Training

An important conception growing out of the last topic is that professional and technical training should be based on scientific knowledge. And Clinton succeeded, along with others, in making provision for such training in institutions. The Mechanic and Scientific Institute is recommended to public patronage because it proposes "imparting the benefits of science to that most useful band of our fellow citizens"—the mechanics. Hence, too, the recommendation of a professorship of agriculture connected with the Board of Agriculture, or attached to the University embracing the kindred sciences of chemistry and geology, mineralogy, botany and other departments of natural history. Hence, too, the recommendation that attendance at the University be made an indispensable passport to medical practise. Even teaching was to be prepared for by a scientific training in so far as that was possible then.   Clinton's viewing with favor the Rensselaer Polytechnic School—certainly one of the most influential schools of applied science in the country—is in line with the foregoing.

Here, too, Clinton was in advance of his time, and when it is remembered that the nineteenth century did not accomplish all he conceived, we should be grateful for the conceptions and for the results accomplished.

EPILOGUE

THE PLACE OF CLINTON IN AMERICAN EDUCATION

The last chapter warrants assigning to Clinton a secure place—and no minor one—in the history of American education. That chapter stated the significance of Clinton's practical influence. He deserves, too, a place as an educational theorist.

Clinton is, of those whose work is finished, perhaps the greatest theorist whose name will be recorded in the future adequate history of American education with the exception of Dr. William T. Harris. We are lauding, even now, as a remarkable contribution to educational theory an educational sociology, and yet here was a man who had formulated in no uncertain terms the fundamental conception of an educational sociology, had seen its implications and had stated them so clearly and so sharply that they would now be matters of current opinion and belief but for their hitherto inaccessible form. It may be urged that Clinton was simply giving expression to what have been called "world views." True, but so did Montaigne and Comenius and Spencer. It is Clinton's great glory that he was the adequate spokesman of his generation—and of the educational implications of the American Revolution. Here is the fullest, clearest, in short, the most adequate expression from the political side of the educational idea which Luther had developed from the religious side.

As a practical reformer, Clinton deservedly ranks with Mann and Barnard in a trinity of educational leadership in American education during the early nineteenth century. He did for New York what Mann did for Massachusetts and Barnard did for Connecticut—and his work, like theirs, was not confined to his own state.

154

Clinton was directly or indirectly responsible for the first step, and several succeeding ones, in the direction of free public schools in New York City; the initiation and the tremendously rapid and beneficent growth of the Lancasterian system; the initiation of the movement for professional training of teachers of New York State; the passage of the first act in which the education of women was promoted by the patronage of government; the beginning of infant schools; the organization and the growth of the State Library during the first decade of its existence, fathering the idea of school district libraries, and encouraging apprentice libraries; the introduction or extension or both of the less formal educational agencies, such as learned societies and lyceums of natural history; the extension of the opportunity for education to the deaf and dumb and other special classes; the construction of a system of juvenile reformation; and the promotion of medical, agricultural and technical education on a scientific basis.

Surely, a similar achievement by almost any other man would have been sufficient to elevate him into the ranks of our foremost educational reformers and formers. But in Clinton's case his achievement in the sphere of education has been overshadowed by his great—though not greater service—in many other spheres. Perceiving that fact it was my purpose to bring into sharp relief the great historical and practical significance of this undeservedly neglected phase of Clinton's service in behalf of his fellow men—a purpose which, I believe, has been realized.

BIBLIOGRAPHY

Manuscript Source Material

Columbia University Library:
De Witt Clinton Papers.
Letter Books, 8 volumes.
Letters to Clinton, 14 volumes.
Miscellaneous Papers, 1 volume.
New York State Education Department:
Minutes of the Board of Regents, 1784-1830.
City Library, City Hall, New York:
Minutes of the Common Council, New York City.
New York Historical Society:
Minutes of the Public School Society, 1817-1830.
Financial Records of the Public School Society, 1805-1830.

Printed Source Material

Addresses of De Witt Clinton:
To Benefactors and Friends of the Free School Society delivered
December, 1809 (New York, 1810).
Introductory Discourse before the Literary and Philosophical Society
of New York, May 4, 1814 (New York, 1815).
Discourse before New York Alpha of Phi Beta Kappa, July 22, 1823
(given in Campbell).
Discourse before the American Academy of Arts, October 23, 1816
(New York, 1816).
Address to the Presbyterian Education Society (given in Hosack's
Memoir of De Witt Clinton).
Address before American Bible Society, May 8, 1823.
Address to the Alumni, Columbia College, May, 1827 (given in
Campbell).
Speeches and Messages to Legislature (given in Senate and Assembly
Journal, 1818-1828).*

---

*Since this work was finished, the State of New York has published the "Messages
from the Governors," edited by Charles Z. Lincoln. Vols. II. and III. contain
Clinton's speeches and messages.

Academician, 1818-19.

Annals of Education, 1831.

CAMPBELL, W. W. Life and Writings of De Witt Clinton (New York, 1849). This contains addresses.

Commercial Advertiser, 1799-1800, New York City.

HOSACK, D. Memoir of De Witt Clinton with an appendix containing documents illustrative of the principal events of his life. (New York, 1829.)

Observations of the Establishment of the College of Physicians and Surgeons in the City of New York. In a letter to James S. Stringham. (New York, 1811.)

HOUGH, F. B. Historical and Statistical Record of the University of the State of New York during the century 1784-1884, with an introductory sketch by David Murray, Secretary of the Board of Regents. (Albany, 1885.)

Laws of New York State, 1784-1857.

Longworth's New York Register and City Directory. 1800-1806.

Jones Directory. (New York City, 1801-1806.)

Munsell's Annals of Albany. 10 vols. (Albany, 1850-59.)

New York State *Assembly* and *Senate Journals*, 1798-1830.

RANDALL, S. S. History of the Common School System of the State of New York from its origin in 1795 to the present time (1871), including the various city and other special organizations and the religious controversies of 1821, 1832, and 1840. (New York and Chicago, 1871.)*

Reports, etc.:

Board of Regents. Annual Reports to the Legislature, 1784.

State Library, New York. Annual Reports to the Legislature, 1818-1830.

New York Institution for the Instruction of Deaf and Dumb. Acts and By-Laws and Reports of the Director. 1831.

New York Public School Society. Annual Reports, 1806-1830.

New York High School Society. Annual Reports, 1825-1828.

Society for the Reformation of Juvenile Delinquents in the City of New York. Annual Reports of the Managers, 1825-1830.

Society of Teachers of the City of New York. Constitution. New York, 1811.

Superintendent of Common Schools Annual Reports, 1814-1828.

---

*For the various other secondary sources see the foot-notes.